PHANTOM
OF THE PINES

PHANTOM
OF THE PINES

MORE TALES OF
THE JERSEY DEVIL

JAMES F. McCLOY & RAY MILLER, JR.

MIDDLE ATLANTIC PRESS
Moorestown, New Jersey

Manufactured in the United States of America

1 2 3 4 5 00 99 98

Library of Congress Cataloging-in-Publication Data

McCloy, James F.
    Phantom of the pines : more tales of the Jersey Devil / James F.
McCloy and Ray Miller, Jr.
        p.   cm.
    ISBN 0-912608-95-1 (alk. paper)
    1. Folklore—New Jersey. 2. Monsters—New Jersey.   I. Miller,
Ray, 1944-   . II. Title.
GR110.N5M324   1998
398.2'09749'0454—dc21   98-13684

Cover design and woodcuts: Laura Shiber
Additional artwork: Jeffrey Filbert
Interior design and composition: Adrianne Onderdonk Dudden

For information write:
Middle Atlantic Press
10 Twosome Drive
P.O. Box 600
Moorestown, NJ 08057

For Charles, Evelyn, Ginger, Karen, Dave, Theresa, and Marissa McCloy
   J.M.

....

For my loving wife, Susan
For Mom and Dad
   R.M., Jr.

CONTENTS

FOREWORD

The Jersey Devil legend is part of the great oral tradition of the state of New Jersey. Some 20 years ago, James F. McCloy and Ray Miller, Jr. wrote the first book-length treatment of this creature, *The Jersey Devil*, which was published by Middle Atlantic Press. It is a tribute to their popular and readable style that the book has remained in print for the past 22 years. During that time, it has found its way into nearly every library in the state, and is widely used by teachers, librarians, and schoolchildren. Whenever the topic of the Jersey Devil comes up, people refer to the book by McCloy and Miller. The authors, both born and raised in New Jersey, have an obvious affection for their subject.

McCloy and Miller could have coasted on the success of *The Jersey Devil*, but they kept collecting stories and anecdotes. Over 20 years of additional effort have yielded a rich harvest of fresh material, which is presented in this second book.

The authors correctly pay homage to their predecessors, but one of the great strengths of this new work is the inclusion of fresh collectanea right up to the 1990s. The authors also write about the opinions and theories of those who pass along these stories.

I am particularly pleased there is a chapter on the Jersey Devil in pop culture. This has been an area of interest to me since coming to

Rutgers University in 1973. In my classes on folklore, I point out that from the colonial days in the Pine Barrens even into the first part of the twentieth century, the Jersey Devil was a creature of mystery and terror. Recently, however, he has been commercialized—and often humanized. McCloy and Miller have thoroughly documented this process.

Phantom of the Pines is a welcome addition to the bookshelves of all those interested in the folklore of New Jersey.

Angus Kress Gillespie

PHANTOM
OF THE PINES

1

MEET THE JERSEY DEVIL

Posses have roamed the Delaware Valley in search of this weird monster. Schools have been closed. Factories have shut down; people have locked themselves inside their houses in fear, sleeping with shotguns, bats, and other weapons at their sides. These events did not occur in the remote past, but in the twentieth century.

The monster has appeared, nightmarishly, face to face with some folks. In 1909, a woman in downtown Philadelphia collapsed when she saw a large, fire-breathing creature in her backyard. In 1951, after a schoolboy had been shocked into screaming at the sight of "It," crowds thronged into the Gibbstown-Paulsboro area when "It" came to haunt again. In 1979, two veteran campers abandoned their campsite one warm night in favor of an all-night diner, because the creature had been besieging them. In 1979 and 1980, the Thing reappeared to overturn trash cans and bang threateningly on houses in Waretown. And every year, campers in the Pine Barrens of New Jersey report otherworldly sounds emanating from the dark heart of the woods.

Many eyewitnesses swear that the monster is real, beyond a doubt. Almost always, they recall overwhelming fear, or shock, at seeing the creature. What they say they have seen does vary with the witness, but they tell of a gargoyle-like creature; others describe a large, anthropoid hairy monster; and there are other frightening renditions as well.

These and similar stories have been circulating in South Jersey since the earliest traditional birthdate of the Jersey Devil, 1735. They originated in a large, somewhat amorphous region known as the Pine Barrens. Its 1700 to 2000 square miles cover roughly one quarter of New Jersey, the most densely populated state in the nation. From Freehold in the north almost to Cape May in the south, and from the Atlantic Coast in the east to within 10 to 15 miles of the Delaware River and Bay in the west, the Pine Barrens include portions of eight of New Jersey's 21 counties. This works out to be an area larger than either Luxembourg or Rhode Island, roughly the size of the entire state of Delaware. Though less than an hour's drive from the New York or Philadelphia metropolitan areas, this region still remains largely untouched forest. Most of the trees are pitch pine, but other varieties, including shortleaf pine, oak, and cedar, are at home there. Much of the land is flat, with some low hills. Cedar swamps are common. Slow-moving, shallow streams tinted brown by cedar and bog iron cross through the region. With the exception of blueberry fields and cranberry bogs, and occasional truck farms, the indigenous sandy soil has largely resisted widespread agriculture, and the iron ore and paper-making industries that once flourished disappeared well before the end of the nineteenth century.

Even today, the region remains sparsely populated. Encroaching urbanization is bringing more residents in, yet the Pine Barrens include huge tracts with no sign of modern civilization. Part of the area remains large, impressive state forests—Wharton, Lebanon, Bass River, and others. Recognizing the ecological importance of this unique area, New Jersey enacted into law the Pinelands Preservation Act, which limits development in large sections of the region.

The original residents of the area, who are descended from colonial English settlers, and, according to tradition, Hessians and some Native Americans, have through the years been given the name "Pineys." Once a term used in a derogatory manner, this epithet has become a source of pride, as symbolized by "Piney Power" t-shirts, buttons, caps, and the like. Recent years have witnessed growing awareness of the history and folk traditions of the people of the Pines, increasing the pride in a Piney heritage.

The Jersey Devil, whose home is usually considered to be the Pines, has roamed South Jersey and neighboring states for over 250 years.

Hundreds of people from all walks of life have seen or heard him, and thousands more have spotted his footprints. Like other demons and creatures of folklore, the Jersey—or Leeds—Devil seems to manifest itself in a number of shapes and sizes, usually some chimerical mixture of animal forms—a deer or a horse with wings, a cow head with a human body, or a dragon that somewhat resembles a dog, goat, fox, cat, various birds, or other creatures. At times, he has appeared in the guise of a large, hairy, Bigfoot-like creature. The traditional description of the Jersey Devil gives him the body of a kangaroo, the head of a dog, red or yellow glowing eyes, the face of a horse, the wings of a bat, the feet of a pig (or the talons of a bird or hooves of a pony), a forked tail, and often horns on his head. He sometimes shoots fire or fetid fumes from his nose or mouth, and is said to be anything from 18 inches in height all the way up to 20 feet, depending on the sighting.

The Jersey Devil traditionally appears to be male. He has been seen hand-in-hand with a beautiful golden-haired girl, or escorting mermaids at sea, and in 1948, one Somerville witness said the Jersey Devil definitely possessed a male anatomy. In 1976, however, letters to several newspapers asserted there was no definite proof of the Jersey Devil's gender. A few reports hold that the Jersey Devil is a female.

Sounds, Acts, and Tracks

The cries the Jersey Devil emits are definitely most memorable, and their reports vary—as do those of his other characteristics. It is not uncommon in the depths of the Pines to hear unidentifiable noises, which people often attribute to the Jersey Devil. Witnesses to the Jersey Devil say once heard, these sounds are never forgotten. They use such terms as "eerie," "weird," "ear-piercing," "bizarre," and "ungodly." Those who have heard them generally call the noises high-pitched, shrill, "like a woman's scream" or "an animal in pain," but some report hearing squawks, whistles, snorts, growls, or grunts.

His actions appear equally varied. Though considered aggressive by some, the Jersey Devil usually flees when encountering humans. Still, through the years, his behavior has shocked many South Jerseyites, who claim the monster has blasted the tops off trees, danced along fence rails, peered frighteningly through windows, boiled fish in streams with his fiery breath, and caused crop failures, sour milk, and droughts.

Like other mysterious monsters, the Jersey Devil leaves behind tracks resembling no other species. Through the years, his footprints have been reported in various sections of New Jersey and elsewhere. A few have proven to be hoaxes, but many remain unexplained. Even experienced hunters, outdoorspeople, and naturalists in the area report encountering tracks they cannot identify. Interestingly enough, the Devil's footprints are often described as relatively small—roughly three inches long and two inches wide. Their conformation is detailed by some as cloven, in the age-old diabolic tradition, but others have seen the prints as circular, much like those of a pony or a horse. Still others perceive them as bear-like, with claws—or bird-like, with talons. In some instances, the creature's prints appeared to reflect some sort of deformity or injury. In a few cases, the prints were rather large and left deep indentations in the ground.

One of the first reports of Devil tracks came from Asa Engle, a South Harrison Township farmer, who recorded in his diary on March 1, 1868, "Great excitement on account of certain tracks resembling those of a mule having been seen in the snow, in various places, some miles distant, which upon being traced mysteriously disappeared in stalk stacks." Witnesses interpreted the tracks as being two-footed.

The Jersey Devil's tracks are perhaps most often associated with a rash of sightings that occurred from January 16th through January 23rd in 1909, when literally thousands of them turned up throughout the Delaware Valley. They appeared in the snow, sometimes covering whole fields. They were spotted on ledges, fence tops, tree branches, roofs, sides of buildings, and a number of inaccessible places. The accounts were many and varied. A Burlington County witness related, "Judging from the different sizes there must have been a whole troupe of. . . 'devils,' as some of the marks were big enough for a horse's hoof; others three inches across or smaller." On Jackson Street in Camden, William Pine's daughter reported seeing strange tracks resembling those of a mule or donkey, but with two limbs, one of which was larger and apparently deformed. In Chester, Pennsylvania, Robert Knott found a number of the Devil tracks near a hennery at Sixth Street and Edgmont Avenue. These tracks ran some 300 feet to the Chester Creek,

negotiating a seven-foot-high board fence. In other places, tracks passed under fence rails only inches from the ground, or slid along a hair's breadth slit between buildings.

Around this period, a photograph of some Jersey Devil tracks was taken by R.C. Archut in Woodbury. This photo remained in the Archut home until a few years ago, when the house was burglarized and the photo disappeared.

Toward the end of January 1909, Jessie N. Rogers, of 13th Street, Hammonton, heard footsteps around his house. At first, he thought his horse had gotten out, but upon investigating he found this was not the case. A few days after that, Rogers found numerous footprints all around his property, which he and his neighbors attributed to the Jersey Devil. Rogers made a plaster cast of a print that had been left in the mud. It was then put on display in the offices of the local newspaper, the *South Jersey Republican*. The cast showed a divided hoof, but one that was smaller and different from that of a horse. In the words of the *South Jersey Republican* that January of 1909, "Nearly all agree that it must have been a two-legged animal, else he used his four feet in a very queer way."

Though 1909 was the banner year for Jersey Devil prints, there have been occasional reports since then, such as in Glassboro in 1913, in Dorothy in 1960, near the Mullica in 1966, and in Batsto in April 1979. Those who live or hunt in the Pine Barrens frequently report unidentifiable tracks in the depths of the forests and cedar swamps.

There were many opinions about the abundance of tracks in 1909. Some people theorized they were from an animal. Many were sure they were from pranksters (though such a number of prints in inaccessible locations would have been very difficult to pull off). Some thought these weird manifestations were the work of evil, diabolic forces and were clearly supernatural; others felt there was nothing supernatural about them. Interestingly, when posses were formed, a number of dogs refused to follow the eerie tracks.

Remedies, Changes in Time, and Perspectives

With the Jersey Devil roaming the Pine Barrens, it was to be expected that innovative minds would create some means to protect against him. According to Renard Wiseman, of New Gretna, folklore recommends throwing salt and pepper around the house. The latter makes him sneeze, and he dislikes salt. While travelling, the best protection is to carry a small bag of onions around the neck. William Kunze, of Ship Bottom, has heard that the only sanctuary from the Jersey Devil is the inside of an outhouse, because the Jersey Devil will not pass through the half-moon cut in the door.

Popular perceptions of the Jersey Devil have changed over the years. In nineteenth-century renditions of the creature, Burlington was often considered the Devil's birthplace. Later, popular belief moved his origin in a southeasterly direction closer to the shore. Today, most people think of his birthplace as Leeds Point both because of the Jersey Devil's association with the Leeds family and the growing popular belief that this coastal village is where the legend started. But Lower Bank, Estellville, and Pleasantville have become frequent variants of the Devil's birthplace in recent years.

Clearly, the Jersey Devil's name has been changed. Following the famous 1909 outbreak of sightings, this change progressed rapidly. Before 1909, the "Leeds Devil" was the name commonly given to the creature. In the various 1909 reports, "Leeds Devil" appears more frequently than "Jersey Devil." Later tales have increasingly contained the term "Jersey Devil." For example, Jack Stackhouse, of Pitman, remembers his grandmother's referring to "The Jersey Devil." Asa Wedding, who lived in Barnegat and Bamber in 1909, also referred to it as "The Jersey Devil," but his grandmother on the Stackhouse side, who lived in Waretown, called it "The Leeds Devil." Luetta Leeds Adams, who was born in Leeds Point, remembers using the term "Leeds Devil" as a child, and recalls the name changing gradually over the years to "Jersey Devil."

The characteristics of the Jersey Devil have undergone a transition as well. In some of the earliest tales, around the eighteenth and early nineteenth centuries, the creature was depicted as much more ferocious. One early story of its birth, for example, depicts the Jersey Devil consuming its family and the midwives in attendance, and then—with a roar—shooting up the chimney and terrorizing the neighborhood. A competing account portrays the unfortunate creature being faithfully cared for by his mother until he escaped a number of years after his birth. In the past, most people expressed real fear of the Jersey Devil, and while some still have that deep trepidation, the Jersey Devil today usually is viewed as a strange phenomenon that arouses more curiosity than fear. The Devil is frequently depicted on postcards, t-shirts, drawings, and posters as a jovial, puckish creature.

With hundreds of years of tradition, it seems somewhat surprising that the Jersey Devil does not have a wider reputation. The Abominable Snowman (or Yeti), Bigfoot, and the Loch Ness monster are internationally known, but to date the Jersey Devil has not received the press notices with which the other creatures have been showered. One reason is that some people erroneously consider him to be indigenous only to the remote Pine Barrens, when the Jersey Devil actually is one of the few monsters to have appeared in heavily urbanized areas. He has been sighted not only in New Jersey, but in Pennsylvania, Maryland, Delaware, New York, California, Texas, and Canada.

A 1976 article in the Philadelphia *Evening Bulletin* argued for more widespread consideration of the Jersey Devil:

> When sober scientific publications from sober institutions such as Harvard and MIT can treat as plausible some evidence of a monster in the depths of Loch Ness, isn't it time that Princeton, Penn, and the other schools of repute hereabouts took a closer look at The Jersey Devil?
>
> We advance this suggestion not from any envy of the better ratings that the Loch Ness monster has received over most other monsters. Newspapers have not always treated the contents of the Scottish lake soberly but they have always treated it with admiration.
>
> But when those Ivy League seats of learning penetrate Scottish mist and myths and concede the possibility of magic there, then it seems to us that the competition had best look to itself.
>
> The Jersey Devil has antecedents that go back to colonial times. It has manifested itself in various guises at various places and times ever since.
>
> Now, if the Pine Barrens of New Jersey will temporarily relinquish any claim they have on the Devil, and if the great seats of learning of the region will make some effort to underwrite the Devil's credentials, and if the Devil itself will take on additional attributes of a denizen from the aquatic depths with appropriate dentistry—well, all that and a few well-timed appearances off Atlantic City might even outdraw casino gambling.

II

ORIGINS

*I*nvestigating the Jersey Devil involves finding seemingly endless versions of when, where, and how he came to be. Tales of the Devil have been enriched by generations of word-of-mouth as well as written acounts, resulting in a number of competing stories. Many versions involve the Leeds family, and specifically Mother Leeds. This dominant tale is firmly rooted in the early history of South Jersey.

People from a number of places in New Jersey believe the Jersey Devil originated in their hometown. According to the most common Devil tales, the claims of some places are greater than those of others, but all these locations have their advocates.

Evesham Township, Southampton Township (in Burlington County), Absecon Island (now Atlantic City), Estellville, and Pleasantville (all three in Atlantic County), Freehold (in Monmouth County), and Vienna (in Warren County) have all, to a greater or lesser degree, been credited as the Jersey Devil's birthplace. Charles Haaf, of Woodstown, even heard the event took place in Philadelphia, but, according to that tale, the Devil preferred to live in the more remote Pine Barrens.

Over the years, Burlington and Leeds Point have been most frequently cited as birthplaces of the Jersey Devil. Lying on the Delaware River midway between Camden and Trenton, Burlington is west of the Pine Barrens. Leeds Point, across the bay from Atlantic City, is on the

Pine Barrens' eastern fringes, where they merge with the salt marshes of New Jersey's coastal bays. These two places bracket the Pine Barrens, home of the Jersey Devil. Most other candidates for the Devil's birthplace lie somewhere in the Pines or marshes between these two locations.

A city of approximately 12,000 people in Burlington County, Burlington is older than Philadelphia, its much bigger neighbor across the Delaware to the south. Rich in history, Burlington boasts many old houses. Its business district, like that of many other old American towns, is undergoing urban renewal to restore historic buildings. About 50 miles southeast of Burlington lies the coastal village of Leeds Point, a lightly populated section of Galloway Township, Atlantic County. In years past, farming, oystering, and fishing were the area's main means of livelihood. By comparison with Burlington's urbanization, Leeds Point remains quiet. A common belief is that the Jersey Devil was born in one of these two places in 1735 and then fled into the Pine Barrens.

Though many towns claim the Jersey Devil was born within their borders, Leeds Point is the chief location in which specific houses are touted as his birthplace. In the 1930s, Mrs. Carrie Bowen, an informant for the writer Henry Charlton Beck, took Beck to a place on Scotts Landing Road and asserted that it was the Shourds house; she claimed the Jersey Devil was born to Mrs. Shourds, not to Mrs. Leeds. This house, along with three other houses on the same road, is one of the four prime candidates for the actual birthsite. All four are now little more than vine-covered foundations in the sandy soil of Leeds Point.

Mrs. Georgiana Blake, another informant to Beck, told him in the 1930s that the Jersey Devil had been born in her town, and that she had narrowed it down to a house that once stood on the 500 block of South Main Street in Pleasantville. An abandoned farmhouse on Retreat Road in Vincentown, Southampton Township, is occasionally pointed out as the spot, as well.

The Larner Leeds house, which until very recently stood on Leeds Point Road, has been named by some people as the birthplace of the Jersey Devil; however, Luetta Leeds Adams, the daughter of Larner Leeds, insists this is not the place. Mrs. Adams says the Leeds Point

Road house came into her family from the Higbees (another old South Jersey family) on her mother's side, not from the Leedses.

The exact year of the Jersey Devil's birth also is a subject of debate. Among the years most frequently given are 1735, 1779, 1800, 1830, 1850, 1855, 1884, and 1887. Some of the later dates can be excluded, however, because written and oral references to the Jersey Devil pre-date them. Far and away, the most commonly held date is 1735.

Stories surrounding the birth are subject to further variation depending on the source or the informant. This kind of interpretation is quite common when a tale is retold over the years. Even so, four major motifs recur in the account of the birth: (1) Mother Leeds curses her own newborn; (2) someone or something else curses Mrs. Leeds' baby; (3) the father is the Devil; (4) a prank is repeated and turns into the Jersey Devil tradition.

The Main Tale and Its Variations

The main tale of the Jersey Devil's birth revolves around Mother Leeds and her unwanted child. Eking out a living in either Burlington or Leeds Point, Mrs. Leeds turned frantic when she realized another child was on the way. This child was her sixth, eighth, tenth, or twelfth (depending on the rendition of the story), but the vast majority say it was the unlucky thirteenth. In anguish at this prospect, she cursed the unborn child—"I am tired of children! Let it be a devil!"

As the legend goes, Mother Leeds was to see the literal fulfillment of her desperate curse. One dark, stormy night, and most of the tellers say in 1735, Mrs. Leeds started labor. Heavy rains pounded the house, and winds blew so hard the candles flickered from the chilly gusts of air squeezing through the shutters. Local midwives gathered around the bed. There are two versions of the frightening event which followed.

According to the less common account, the child was born a devil baby, already a grotesque creature. More commonly, the story goes that a normal baby boy was delivered, but within a few moments the child began a rapid metamorphosis in front of the startled onlookers. As the horrific change began to occur, Mr. Leeds and the Leeds children rushed into the room to see what was happening. The baby's body

lengthened tremendously, forming into a long, serpentine shape with a pointed Devil's tail. Its hands and feet turned into hooves and claws. Its pink, chubby baby face coarsened into the long, bony structure of a horse's head. Bat wings sprang from its shoulder blades, and two horns emerged from its skull.

Then the thing stood up, larger and more powerful than a full-grown man, and bellowed louder than the crashing thunder outside. The walls shook from the sound. His tail thrashed about faster and faster. Then the beast sprang on the roomful of his unfortunate victims. After devouring some and beating others senseless with his tail, he let out another unearthly roar and flapped his huge wings as he flew up the chimney, sending a noisy wake of dust and bricks into the fire as he made his escape into the night.

A similar account, and one of the earliest written versions of the birth of the Jersey Devil, appeared in the May 1859 *Atlantic Monthly*. W.F. Mayer, of New York, recounted his fall 1858 visit to the area around Hanover Iron Works, Burlington County. Mayer questioned his friend, Mr. B., because he had been hearing about it locally. Mr. B. then replied at length:

> There lived, in the year 1735, in the township of Burlington, a woman. Her name was Leeds, and she was shrewdly suspected of a little amateur witch-craft. Be that as it may, it is well established, that, one stormy, gusty night, when the wind was howling in turret and tree, Mother Leeds gave birth to a son, whose father could have been none other than the Prince of Darkness. No sooner did he see the light than he assumed the form of a fiend, with a horse's head, wings of bat, and a serpent's tail. The first thought of the newborn Caliban was to fall foul of his mother, whom he scratched and bepummelled soundly, and then flew through the window out into the village, where he played the mischief generally. Little children he devoured, maidens he abused, young men he mauled and battered; and it was many days before a holy man succeeded in repeating the enchantment of Prospero. At length, however, Leed's devil was laid,—but only for one hundred years.
>
> During an entire century, the memory of that awful monster was preserved, and, as 1835 drew nigh, the denizens of Burlington and the Pines looked trembling for his rising. Strange to say, however, no one but Han-

nah Butler has had a personal interview with the fiend; though, since 1835, he has frequently been heard howling and screaming in the forest at night, to the terror of the Rats in their lonely encampments. Hannah Butler saw the devil, one stormy night, long ago; though some skeptical individuals affirm, that very possibly she might have been led, under the liquid Jersey lightning, to invest a pine-stump, or, possibly, a belated bear, with diabolical attributes and a Satanic voice. However that may be, you cannot induce a Rat to leave his hut after dark,—nor, indeed, will you find many Jerseymen, though of a higher order of intelligence, who will brave the supernatural terrors of the gloomy forest at night, unless secure in the strength of numbers.

The term "Pine Rats" referred to in Mr. B's account was a derogatory term for the residents of the Pines. Mayer found the belief in the Jersey Devil to be quite widespread among the various social elements of the region, and this account is one of the first to pinpoint the year of the Devil's birth at 1735.

Still another rendition of the birth of the Jersey Devil has the monster kept under close cover by Mother Leeds once she saw that her child was grotesquely different, and a third interesting 1735 tale is told by Peggy Dorsey, of Ocean City, who says that it was Mother Leeds' thirteenth child. The woman was weakened from multiple childbirths, afflicted with failing eyesight, and getting on in years. Because of her vision problem, Mother Leeds would not confine the child but walked about the area with her strange offspring, unaware of any deformity. The child's little blue coat, which flapped as he moved around with childish energy, soon became confused with bat wings. As the child grew, however, now even his mother realized he was not like her other children. Mrs. Leeds continued to care for the child, but she also kept him locked in the attic or the cellar. Then, one night, 4 to 20 years after the birth, a violent storm swept through the area. Perhaps the strong winds blew open the cellar door or attic window, from which the Devil child then fled, or it may have flown up the chimney. In any case, the creature escaped. The Jersey Devil haunted the area so much after he was free that in the 1740s, a clergyman exorcised the spirit for a hundred years, by means of bell, book, and candle.

Another interesting version of the main tale claims Mrs. Leeds and her husband lived in Evesham. The Mrs. Leeds in this rendition was

Ann Archer Leeds. An anonymous elderly gentleman gave a vivid account of it to the *Newark Sunday Call* in 1887, prefacing his recounting with, "I can only tell you the story as it has come down through the generations from over a hundred years ago. You may believe it or not, as you please, but you may walk a good ways around that section of country before you will find anyone who doubts it. . . . The granddaughter of the woman who was Mrs. Leeds' nurse is still living in Burlington County, she says the story I shall tell you has been handed down without change or addition."

Ann Archer, he related, was a "holy terror," a lively 19-year-old who moved with her family into the Evesham area at about the close of the American Revolution. She was the life of the party at all the cornhuskings, apple-paring bees, and other social events; and her reputation was known for miles around. Ann had little regard for anyone but herself. She exhibited a violent temper when she did not get her way. The community was "struck dumb" when Ann Archer married Robert Leeds, a local schoolteacher, who was known to be "the steadiest, quietest, and most respectable man" in the neighborhood.

Robert Leeds thought he could "tame" Ann, but she refused to settle down despite her husband's protests. When the rebellious girl learned she was with child, she became increasingly wilder—right up until the night before the child was born. A nurse was called in, who claimed that "on that eventful night Mrs. Leeds raised her hands above her head and shrieked: 'I hope it will be a devil!'" The next night, this nurse appeared pale and in great terror, as she reported, "Mrs. Leeds is a mother! But her offspring was a hideous deformity, and flew up and out of the chimney, shrieking and screaming as it went!"

The reaction of the people in Evesham was incredulity. They suspected that the nurse had assisted Mrs. Leeds somehow in getting rid of the child. Their opinion soon changed, however, when a panicked hunter returned from the nearby woods "terrified into jelly," saying that he had seen a "hideous creature which had scared him cold by its terrible shrieks, which were like no other noise he could possibly imagine, and possessed an amount of concentrated horror impossible to imagine." Soon others began to see it as well. The descriptions all matched that originally reported by the nurse, and the Jersey Devil was accepted as a frightening part of the Evesham woods.

The Evesham description portrayed the Jersey Devil as three feet high, with the body and limbs of a large child and large powerful wings, a round, owl-like head, and a diabolic human face featuring large, round, shining eyes. But the creature was reported to be "beautifully feathered," with a black dot near the tip of each feather. The Devil could not talk, but whenever someone got too near, it yelled in a horrifying way.

Ann Archer Leeds was changed by the birth of her devil child. Her wild ways and bad temper disappeared, and she became a model wife. The pressure of these experiences proved too much for the couple, though, and they moved to Pennsylvania and a new life, leaving their devil child to haunt the woods of Evesham.

Atlantic City (then called Absecon Island) has its own rendering of the main tale, but the age of this version is in question. It could, in fact, be a modern invention. According to this tale, sometime in the 1800s, Mrs. Leeds gave birth to a misshapen devil child who roamed about the house from the time of its infancy. This devil child was evil incarnate, and it viciously struck out at anyone who got near it, even its mother, who loved the unfortunate creature. One day, when the window was inadvertently left open, the creature fled the house and took up residence among the sand dunes. The family attempted many times to recapture it, but to no avail. With maternal devotion, Mother Leeds ventured forth each day to the dunes to feed the creature, and each day she returned home bleeding and with her clothes torn from the claws of the diabolic child. She continued to do this despite the pleas of her family. As to when this self-sacrificing nursing activity ceased, however, the Atlantic City tale is silent.

Someone Else Curses the Child

Another account of the Jersey Devil's birth involves not Mother Leeds cursing the child, but someone—or something—else cursing Mrs. Leeds' child. A patriotic version relates the affair of a Leeds Point girl with a British soldier—or, in some versions, a Hessian. The affair in question took place around October 1778, during a British invasion of the area that culminated in the battle of Chestnut Neck. The American girl was cursed with a devil baby through some apparently patriotic

American metaphysical agency as a punishment for her treasonous behavior.

In another curse tale, sometime during 1850, a young South Jersey girl was frightened by a gypsy who asked for food. When the girl refused to supply it, the gypsy cursed her next child.

A third variation of the curse involves a Protestant clergyman who visited the Leeds family, who were known in their neighborhood as rowdies who shunned churchgoing. After the family rebuffed the clergyman's attempts at their conversion, Mrs. Leeds gave birth to the Jersey Devil.

A different twist on the religious angle goes that a salesman was travelling door to door, offering Sacred Heart of Jesus images, when a violently anti-Catholic woman shouted at him she would rather have a devil in her house than one of these icons. The child she was expecting at the time—of course—turned out to be the Jersey Devil.

Satan as the Father

Occasionally, as in Mayer's 1859 account, the tellers of the Jersey Devil's origin insist that the father of the child is the Devil himself. This third variation of the main tale has in some of its yarns that the father is "The Prince of Darkness," "Beelzebub," or one of the Devil's other monikers. Along with this attribution of paternity, in some accounts, is the theory that Mother Leeds engaged in some sort of mysterious practices of witchcraft or the occult.

The Jersey Devil from a Prank

In the least common accounts of its birth, the Jersey Devil is a fictitious character who resulted from a prank. There are a handful of people who insist it was one of their friends or relatives who started the whole legend in recent times. One woman, for example, said in 1973, "The Jersey Devil? My husband started the Jersey Devil story when he was a teenager. Nobody can tell me any different."

The most common prankster story has been passed down since Halloween of 1830, when it was supposedly started by John Vliet, a New Jersey Assemblyman from Warren County. According to historical records, a Daniel Vliet of Warren County served in the New Jersey Assembly in 1828–29. Whether Vliet was the Vliet of Jersey Devil fame, though, is still an open question.

In early October 1830, Vliet (or sometimes spelled Vleit) travelled to New York to shop and while walking along Broadway, he noticed some strange masks on display. Intrigued, he purchased the most frightful one and took it home to Vienna. After Vliet and his family tired of the mask, he passed it on to Jack Sutton, a farmhand. Shortly thereafter, the Jersey Devil began to appear.

One night, Squire Fleming, who was walking by Whitesell's Corner on the outskirts of Vienna (the area is now called Great Meadows), felt something pulling his coattails. He wheeled around and screamed because confronting him was a thing with a hideous face. It also was wearing a white robe. Fleming ran for all he was worth, crashed through the doors of the Great Meadows Inn, and collapsed in exhaustion. Squire Fleming was a respected member of the community and a pillar of the church. The local residents were aghast as Fleming vividly retold his experience, and one of the listeners dubbed the mysterious visitor the "Jersey Devil."

Concern was at its height when Morris Cummins was confronted next, again at Whitesell's Corner. Cummins had the habit of asking questions aloud to himself as he walked along; one night, he was flabbergasted to hear answers coming from a few feet behind him. His actions were the same as Fleming's, except that Cummins raced to the Vienna Hotel, down the other way.

The threat posed by this particular Jersey Devil legend was rapidly deflated when the next Vienna resident to be victimized turned out to be Richard Hall, a strong and fearless carpenter. Hall was returning from the Vliet farm, where he had done some work, when the "beast" jumped from the bushes and began barking like a dog. Unlike the others, Hall stood his ground, seized a piece of fence rail, and pummeled his adversary, who cried out, "Don't kill me! I'm Jack Sutton!" After a few more swings, Hall walked off, leaving the stunned Sutton on the ground.

Sutton fled the area, never to be seen again, and a torn-up false face and sheet were found at Whitesell's Corner.

Double Trouble

One tale claims the Jersey Devil had a twin. This story no longer enjoys the popularity it once did, but Herbert Halpert found evidence of this twin tale while doing fieldwork in rural Burlington County in the 1940s for his doctoral dissertation, "Folktales and Legends from the New Jersey Pines: A Collection and a Study." Elvin Sweet, James D. Eastlaw, and Mrs. Henry Parks told Halpert they had heard the Jersey Devil was actually the survivor of a pair of twins. In one version, both children were Devils. In another, one child was a Devil and one was normal. One of the twins was smothered, but the other escaped from home to lead its mysterious life thereafter.

This odd tale surfaced again in a letter to E. Burke Maloney, of the *Asbury Park Press*, in 1967. Postmarked Linwood, New Jersey, the letter was anonymous, signed only with the epithet "One Who Knows." The spellings are a direct quote.

> I have been reading the storys about him in the Atlantic City papers since I was very young. None of them have been all true.
>
> The Leed's Devil was a twin. . . when she was expecting again she said she hoped to God this thime it would be twins and both be devils. She had twin boys they smothered one to death between featherbeds. The other one got away. All at the time were so shocked at the terrible sight they couldn't catch him. He went out the window.
>
> I know this is a true story as my grandmother delivered them. She said they were very hard to hold. She said there toes and fingers were very long (know tail). They had wings on their Shoulder blades. There eyes were large and close together.

The Leeds Family

The Jersey Devil is almost always mentioned in conjunction with the Leeds family of South Jersey. Across the United States, this principal family now numbers in the thousands, including many who have remained close to their region of original settlement. Represented by statesmen, monarchs, inventors, landholders, educators, and businessmen, the Leeds family has been in America for over 300 years, but its origins can be traced back to early England. Some of the earliest members of the family were descendents of Cedric, King of Wessex, circa the sixth century.

Thomas Leeds was the first family member to migrate to the New World. Fleeing the political and religious turmoil of seventeenth-century England, he departed from Leeds, England in 1676 and settled in Shrewsbury, Monmouth County, where he obtained 240 acres from the East Jersey Proprietors. His son, Daniel, arrived in Burlington two years later, aboard the *Shield*. Daniel, perhaps the most famous of the Leedses, is the progenitor from whom most of the Leedses in America trace their heritage.

Daniel Leeds rapidly succeeded in America. As early as 1682, he became a member of the Assembly, and later served in the Council. In 1687, he became the first Surveyor General of West Jersey, and in the 1690s, he obtained a land grant from the West Jersey Proprietors for a section in the Great Bay area. Within that area, the family settled in Leeds Point. Until 1708, Daniel Leeds served on the New Jersey Council under Edward Hyde, Lord Cornbury, Governor of New York and New Jersey. He left political life in 1708, when Lord Cornbury was recalled to England.

Daniel Leeds' *The American Almanack* may have been the first such work published in America. It first appeared in 1687, and Daniel continued it until 1716, when his sons, Titan and Felix, took it over. Leeds' *Almanack* played an important part in helping to launch Benjamin Franklin's *Poor Richard's Almanac,* when a lively competition ensued between the two, described by some historians as a "good-natured exchange" and by others as a relatively acerbic "war of letters."

The Leeds family continued to prosper and remain politically influential. In 1783, Jeremiah Leeds became Atlantic City's first permanent settler. Near where casinos now stand, Leeds erected a log cabin, called "Leeds' Plantation," where he grew rye and corn. In 1839, Millie, Jeremiah's widow, expanded her house into a hotel and tavern—the first in the area. As the resort grew through the nineteenth century, the Leeds family continued to play a prominent role in its development. When Atlantic City was incorporated in 1854, its first mayor was Chalkley S. Leeds.

What caused such a distinguished, influential family to be associated with the infamous Jersey—or Leeds—Devil? Possibly some people were jealous of the family's success, politics, or social position, just as some historians feel that such mechanisms were at work in the Salem witch trials. Daniel Leeds, the patriarch himself, was involved in controversy as well. The Quakers strongly disapproved of his *Almanack* for being critical of certain religious practices. Leeds ended up withdrawing from the Society of Friends, though his son Japhet later rejoined. This religious controversy somehow might have linked "the Devil" with Leeds' unpopularity with the Quakers.

Before modern advances in medical and mental services, physical or psychological abnormalities created extreme problems for any family in which they occurred. It has been theorized that a deformed child was born to the Leeds family, and that this unfortunate youngster was referred to as the "Jersey Devil." In those days, an abnormal child often was associated with the Devil.

One story supporting this speculation holds that William Leeds (brother of the famous Daniel and son of Thomas) married Dorothea in England and was one of the first Leedses to make the move to America. William and his family settled in Monmouth County, though later in life he moved south to Little Egg Harbor. The couple had six children, and their fourth child, Daniel, suffered from some sort of mental deficiency. Daniel's older brother, William Jr., who remained in the Middletown, Monmouth County area, referred to Daniel in his will as "my weak minded and helpless brother Daniel Leeds" and repeatedly insisted that executors of the will take care of the property left to Daniel. Quite interestingly, the date of William Jr.'s will regarding his "helpless" brother is June 20, 1735—the traditional year of the birth of the Jersey Devil.

In addition to outsiders making fun of the unfortunate child, troubles within the Leeds family could have caused the criticism of Daniel to escalate into a full-blown Devil legend. There are records of some family land disputes.

How does the Leeds family view their relationship with the Jersey Devil today? Such a widespread and diverse family naturally produces a variety of opinons. Quite a few Leedses tend to downplay the whole thing. "Nonsense," says one Leeds, who no doubt speaks for many.

Native American Influences

Some feel the Jersey Devil antedates the colonial period of history that usually corresponds to his birthtime, and they suggest that the seeds of the legend go back to the Delaware (or Lenni Lenape) tribe of Native Americans, New Jersey's original inhabitants. This is conceivable, for as the white man moved into New Jersey and the Native Americans moved out, there was obviously some rich intercultural communication. Did the white man bring the Jersey Devil with him, or did he build on a pre-existing legend?

One possible answer may be found in certain place names within New Jersey. Two of the most likely to show Native American influence on the Jersey Devil are "Shamong" and "Squanqum." Shamong Township, Burlington County, is in the heart of the Pine Barrens, the traditional home of the Jersey Devil. The word *Shamong* comes from the Lenape, meaning "horn" or "horn place." Though many believe the name refers to the many deer found in the area, others maintain that the horns speak of a strange creature frequenting the territory. There are two Squanqums in New Jersey, one a location near Allaire State Park in Monmouth County and the other a brook in Gloucester County. One of the translations of *Squanqum* is "place of the evil god," which leads some to wonder if something unusual occurred in these locations well before the whites set foot in the area.

One curious story, for example, comes by way of the Swedes' interaction with the Native Americans, and it is recorded in Mickles' *Reminiscences of Old Gloucester County* (1845). On the shores of the Delaware the Swedes often found what one old Swedish author called "a *rattle snake,* which has a head like that of a dog and *can bite off a man's leg as clear as if it had been hewn down with an axe!*" Stories of these snakes, which were sought by Native American women as some sort of medicine for pregnancy, were often told around this time.

Another birth legend is tied directly to the Native Americans. In the late 1970s, Doug Norcross, a student at Cook College, Rutgers University, told Alice Nicholson, of Douglass College, this account: "The Jersey Devil is a direct descendent of an old Lenape Indian that put a curse upon his wife because she allowed a white man to sleep with her. She got pregnant and the son was the original Jersey Devil. The current

Devil is his great-great-great (something like that) grandson of that illegitimate child."

If the Jersey Devil can be said to have Native American origins, perhaps the most interesting legend along these lines is that of the *Mising* (or *Misinghalikun*), a deity of the Lenni Lenape (or Delaware) Native American pantheon. In his *Religion and Ceremonies of the Lenape*, M.R. Harrington discusses the *Mising*, a sky god whose function was largely to be the protector of crops, wildlife, and children. Several features of this belief and of the ceremonies associated with it might be forerunners of the legend of the Jersey Devil.

The Delawares had an annual spring ceremony that featured the *Mising*, to ensure their crops and game flourished for another year. They danced and sang all night around a fire, over which venison and hominy were cooked for the morning-after feast. The highlight of this ceremony was the *Mising* himself, impersonated by an agile member of the tribe, who leapt and danced throughout the festivities—jumping over dancers, fences, and the fire.

Harrington cites the report of an early witness who recounts what he saw at a *Mising* ceremony:

> After the dance is underway the Messinq comes from the darkness, jumps over the dancers, and dances between the other dancers and the fire. He makes some funny and queer gestures, kicks the fire, and then departs. The Messinq is never allowed to talk. . . He never thinks of climbing a fence, but jumps over it every time that one is in the way. The Devil Dance is what the white men call it, but the Delawares call it the Messinq, or "solid face" dance. The Messinq does not represent an evil spirit, but is always considered a peacemaker. I suppose that it is from his hideous appearance that white men call him the devil.

This account is from a traveller who was well ahead of most white settlers. He describes the *Mising* as "hideous" no doubt because he saw no European parallel. The *Mising* impersonator wore a mask, usually carved from wood, but sometimes cut from stone or molded from clay. It was unusually large, with huge features and a neutral or plain expression. The right half was painted red, and the left half painted black. The impersonator would be covered in a bearskin costume, complete with leggings and a cap, so that no human features could be seen. The oddity of this dress clearly appeared frightening to the observer quoted here, and it probably was seen this way by many early settlers.

To the Native Americans, the *Mising* was a protector deity who had to be worshipped to prevent natural calamities such as storms or earthquakes, and its function with children took place throughout the year. If a Delaware child misbehaved or was sick, the family summoned the *Mising* impersonator for a visit. They believed an appearance by this strange god-like person was enough to correct the problem. Native American parents threatened naughty children with comments like, "If you don't behave, *Mising* will carry you off in a bag full of snakes."

There are clearly certain parallels between the *Mising* and the Jersey Devil, who at times appeared as a hairy creature walking on its hind legs, reminiscent of the *Mising* ritual costume. Virtually the only god that the Delawares attempted to impersonate, the *Mising* represented the only strange creature fashioned by the Native Americans the early white settlers might have seen. In an already alien culture, European settlers observing this creature would have been frightened, and, because of the fear, the *Mising* ceremony was often called the "Devil Dance" by whites. Both the Jersey Devil and the *Mising* have been associated with storms and calamities, as well as with animals and nature. Added to a number of other Native American supernatural deities, the *Mising* belief might have carried substantial weight in the creation of the Jersey Devil tradition.

III

A SURVEY OF THE JERSEY DEVIL'S HISTORY

From the traditional birthdate in 1735 all the way up to the present day, Jersey Devil incidents have been reported regularly. During this time, however, there were many periods, each spanning years, when there were no reports of Devil activity. Some people even announced the "demise" of the Jersey Devil.

Many of the eighteenth- and nineteenth-century references to this strange phenomenon are somewhat sketchy. In the twentieth century more detailed information became available, so the Jersey Devil and his activities are better known. A look at some high points through the centuries provides an interesting view of the nature of the Jersey Devil. Some of these references have been passed along in print, and others are based on oral folktales of this strange monster.

One early written reference to the Jersey Devil was from the diary of Vance Larner, a woodsman who lived in what is now Lebanon State Forest. Writing in October 1790, Larner sketched his first-hand observation of this strange entity: "It was neither beast, nor man, nor spirit, but a hellish brew of all three. It was beside a pond when I came upon it. I stopped and did not move. Nay, I could not move. It was dashing its tail to and fro in the pond and rubbing its horns against a tree trunk. It was as large as a moose with leather wings. It had cloven hooves as big around as an oak's trunk. After it was through with the tree, it yielded an awful scream as if it were a pained man, and then flew across the pond until I could see it no more."

Some Early Sightings and Activities

That the Jersey Devil was quite well known in the eighteenth century is exemplified by a crowd of 40,000 that gathered at Walnut and Sixth Streets in Philadelphia on January 9, 1793, to see Frenchman Jean-Pierre Blanchard and his dog make the first balloon flight in America. President George Washington was on hand and, not knowing where Blanchard might land, presented him with a letter of introduction. The hydrogen-filled balloon lifted off and after reaching an altitude of one mile sailed across the Delaware River and landed outside of Woodbury, New Jersey, 45 minutes later.

According to legend, Jersey farmers mistook the balloon for the Jersey Devil and were prepared to blast it to pieces with their guns. However, Blanchard avoided disaster when he presented his letter from Washington and passed around some French wine. He arrived back safely in Philadelphia a few hours later.

Throughout the nineteenth century, the Jersey Devil made sporadic appearances, either in the Pine Barrens or in the vicinity of the Jersey Shore. He has been associated in legend with two famous historic figures from that time as well. In one popular tale, Commodore Stephen Decatur was testing cannon balls at the Hanover Iron Works when he saw the Jersey Devil flying across the range. Decatur fired on the creature, scoring a direct hit, but the Devil appeared unscathed and, to Decatur's amazement, continued to fly across the range—and out of sight. The Devil's other brush with the famous came when Joseph Bonaparte, former King of Spain and brother of Napoleon, was hunting and encountered the creature. Bonaparte lived in Bordentown from 1816 to 1839, following his brother's downfall.

During the late 1830s and early 1840s, the Jersey Devil busied himself howling in one particular section of the Pine Barrens, much to the discomfort of its residents. The unusually high number of missing livestock was considered the work of the Devil. In the 1880s and '90s, the Devil seemed to concentrate on the Shore area near Atlantic City. He was sighted in Absecon, Smithville, Long Beach Island, Brigantine Beach, and Leeds Point. So familiar was he to this area that the heavy storms that battered Atlantic City in January 1884 were attributed by some residents to an angered Jersey Devil. Interestingly enough, his last appearance in the nineteenth century was in Spring Valley, New York, where he crossed the path of George Saarosy, who described Jersey's famous demon as a "flying serpent."

The Phenomenal Week in 1909

As mentioned earlier, the most sustained series of Jersey Devil sightings happened one snowy week in 1909, from January 16th to 23rd. This is one of the rare instances in modern times when a supernatural creature alarmed an entire region. Residents of New Jersey, Pennsylvania, and Delaware, where the Jersey Devil appeared a host of times during this phenomenal week, all reacted to these strange happenings.

Some people locked themselves in their houses. Posses combed the snowy woods and fields searching for this mysterious intruder, and trolleys in Trenton and New Brunswick sported armed guards. Bristol, Pennsylvania, and Camden, New Jersey, police fired at the creature, and one person claimed to have wounded it. School closed in Mount Ephraim, and the Taggart School in Philadelphia had an appreciable decline in attendance. Mills in Gloucester and Hainesport were closed because workers failed to report, and a Camden theatre had so few patrons that the show did not go on. The only places where people seemed willing to go were the churches, which enjoyed a brisk increase in attendance following an extra-heavy rash of footprint sightings in Pitman.

Not everyone was frightened by tales of the Jersey Devil, however. Some people felt it was caused by an abundant apple jack crop in New Jersey. Others scoffed at the whole thing.

Thack Cozzens, of Woodbury, is perhaps the first recorded eyewitness to the events of that eerie week. The night of Saturday the 16th, Cozzens had a frightening encounter with the Jersey Devil, who appeared as a strange creature, emitting steam. This monstrous being flew across the street and, before it disappeared, looked back with phosphorescent eyes, which Cozzens called "the eyes of the beast." That same night, the Jersey Devil made a number of appearances in Bristol, where Patrolman James Sackville shot at him.

At first, people did not seem to associate the prints that frequently appeared that week with the Jersey Devil, but by the end of the week, all save the skeptics were willing to admit the creature was roaming the area. Decades later, people still vividly recall seeing or hearing about these weird footprints.

Elizabeth Harrison, of Collingswood, remembers what happened to her uncle. He had always been an advocate of fresh air and insisted everyone in the family open the windows at night, no matter how cold it was. That custom came to an abrupt halt after Harrison's uncle found Jersey Devil footprints on his windowsill. In fact, family legend holds he never again allowed a raised window at night.

In 1973, Elizabeth Dannenhower, of Haddonfield, reminisced to the authors about that week: "I remember it as clearly as if it were yesterday. They weren't footprints, but they were lines in the snow circling the house, and my mother told me they were the marks of the Jersey Devil."

Watson Buck, of Rancocas, typified the reactions of many of those who saw the prints when he told us, "I'm over 80, but I remember as if it was yesterday the night a mysterious creature appeared right outside my window. It was a cold, snowy night in the winter of 1909. I was sleeping in a little bungalow in Masonville. Suddenly something outside the place woke me up. The thing stopped at the window and if I could only have pulled the curtain back I could have seen it. But I was too sleepy. The next morning I went outside and there they were—tracks in the snow at my window and all around the house, tracks of a four-footed animal. I've been doing research on the Jersey Devil for over 60 years now, and those tracks are still a mystery. Behind every tradition, you know, there's something real."

During the rash of sightings that week, Mr. and Mrs. Nelson Evans, of Gloucester City, got a good look at the Devil as he walked around the roof of their shed for a full ten minutes late one night. The terrified Evanses noticed the traditional attributes of the Jersey Devil. Evans told a local paper the three-and-a-half-foot-tall creature had "a head like a collie dog and a face like a horse. . . . It had a long neck, wings about two feet long, and its back legs were like those of a crane, and it had horse's hooves. It walked on its back legs and held up two short front legs with paws on them." Evans managed to shoo it away but said that the departing creature "turned around, barked at me, and flew away." Hundreds of the curious flocked to the home the next day, where Evans gave escorted tours to his shed.

Adam Rouner also got a good view of the creature at the State Arsenal in Trenton and drew a sketch of what he saw. Rouner's drawing depicts a horse with wings, sporting horns on his head, and an alligator tail. There's no explanation of why he included mountains in the background, though, because the Trenton vicinity is fairly flat.

One of the most bizarre episodes during this week occurred around 1:00 A.M. on January 21st, at the Black Hawk Social Club in Camden. A Mr. Rouh heard "an uncanny sound" at the back window. Staring in was a frightening creature, whose appearance drove the Social Club members out the door "in abject fear," with Rouh taking up a bludgeon in self-defense. As Rouh told in his account to a local newspaper, the sounds of the Jersey Devil as it flew away were "blood curdling."

About an hour later the Devil buzzed a Public Service Railway trolley in Haddon Heights. The first passenger to spot the creature cried out, "There's that thing, take it away!" After the ordeal was over, the trolley conductor, Lewis Boeger, gave this description: "In general appearance it resembles a kangaroo. . . It has a long neck and from what glimpse I got of its head its features are hideous. It has wings of a fairly good size and of course in the darkness looked black."

Maybe the Jersey Devil had an affinity for trolleys. Edward Davis, a trolley car operator in Burlington, saw something that "looked like a winged kangaroo with a long neck" dart across the tracks in front of him.

Reports of strange happenings continued to pour in from throughout the Delaware Valley. Chickens mysteriously disappeared, and after weird cries in the night were heard, many of the poultry in Bridgeton and Millville were found dead. They had no marks on them. A Westville women's club abandoned their meeting when the Jersey Devil happened by, and an unidentified Burlington policeman was quoted as saying the creature "had no teeth; its eyes were like blazing coals."

Two of the most spectacular appearances the Jersey Devil made during this week of phenomenal events occurred in West Collingswood and Camden. According to Alfred Heston in his book *Jersey Waggon Jaunts,* the West Collingswood incident began when Charles Klos and George Boggs were walking down Grant Avenue and saw what appeared to be an ostrich perched on the roof of the fire chief's home. Klos and Boggs called the fire department, who on arrival turned a hose on the Jersey Devil. This blasted the creature about 50 yards down the street. The Jersey Devil soon rallied, however, and charged the firemen, who in turn attempted to stop the Devil's charge by throwing sticks and stones—to no avail. The melee continued until the creature flew over their heads and disappeared.

The Camden episode involved Mrs. Mary Sorbinski, who lived on Mount Ephraim Avenue. When she heard loud, strange noises in her back yard, Mary seized a broom and ran out the back door to find her pet dog in the "vise-like grip" of a "horrible monster." With all her might, Mary swung the broom at the creature, who dropped the dog and, emitting sounds that resembled a combination of the "hoot of an owl" and the "snarl of a hyena," nearly struck Mrs. Sorbinski in its escape. After carrying her wounded pet into the house, Mary began screaming. Her cries attracted a large crowd, which included the Camden police. Suddenly the crowd heard high-pitched screams from atop the standpipe on Kaighn Hill, and Patrolmen Thomas Cunningham and William Crouch ran toward the noises with the crowd at their heels. The officers emptied their revolvers at the creature, but once again the Devil disappeared into the night.

As the week ran out, so apparently did the Jersey Devil's visit. To date, that week in January 1909 remains the period in which the creature elicited the most attention. Why, however, remains a mystery.

From 1909 to the Present

From 1909 to the present, the Jersey Devil has continued to appear. As a young boy in 1911, Captain David Higbee, of Haddonfield, who would later spend many years on ships, saw one of the strangest sights of his life in what is now Barrington. "Late in the afternoon on a Saturday in mid-February, my brother and I saw small hoofprints in the snow near my aunt's home. We followed these prints down to a creek on the edge of the woods. There on the bank of the creek was this animal. It was the size of a small pony, with a head somewhat like a horse, but its body was very long and it had a shaggy fur coat. Its legs were short. As we fearfully approached, it jumped the creek and disappeared into the woods."

A Vineland resident reports that his father also saw the Jersey Devil around this time. "My father, who was born in 1896, saw the Jersey Devil when he was a boy. He was driving a horse and wagon along a road near Vineland, when the horse just stopped and it got very hot. There on the road in front of him was the Jersey Devil. It was a figure about four or five feet tall and glowing red all over. After a moment the Devil ran away."

In the 1920s, there were several notable appearances typical of this strange monster, where he came out of nowhere, frightened someone, and then disappeared again. Around 1927, a taxi driver heading toward Salem late one night was forced to stop to repair a flat tire. Just as he finished, his taxi began to shake violently. There, "something that stood upright like a man but without clothing and covered with hair" had its huge hands on his vehicle. He jumped into the taxi and sped off in fright, abandoning the jack and flat tire and not stopping until he reached Salem, where he told his harrowing story to Edward R. Jones and Bill Reed, who bravely drove out to have a look for themselves, leaving the shaken taxi driver back in town. Jones and Reed retrieved the flat tire, but the Jersey Devil had once again melted back into the surrounding woods.

Berry pickers in both Mays Landing and Leeds Point encountered the Jersey Devil in July 1930. One Mays Landing motorist reported that a completely terrified man attempted to jump into his car, claiming the Jersey Devil was pursuing him. At about the same time that day, Howard Marcey and John Huntzinger observed the Jersey Devil not far from their homes in Erial; they said the beast had the "body of a man, head of a cow, large bat-like wings, big feet, and flew up in the air, and then cut the tops off trees." Strangely, the two men's daughters saw the same thing at exactly the same place some unspecified time after that.

On a hot summer day in 1934 around Iona Lake in rural Gloucester County, a group of boys found large, cloven footprints on a gravel road. They rushed to alert their families, and half a dozen men armed with sticks and accompanied by a state trooper combed the area, where they found additional footprints and mysteriously broken branches. Other sightings from the 1930s have been recorded. Philip Smith alleged that he saw the Jersey Devil walking down a street in Woodstown in 1935, and it looked something like a large German Shepherd dog.

In late November 1951, something of a public flap occurred with the Jersey Devil in the Gibbstown-Paulsboro area. It began one night when a ten-year-old boy looked out the window of the Dupont Clubhouse in Gibbstown. There, staring back at him, was a horrible creature with "blood coming out of its face." The unfortunate boy collapsed in a fit of screams; according to *The Record,* he "fell to the floor, and his body was wracked by spasms." The chaperone and other children, at first not believing his story, managed to calm him down. That same night, however, when he saw the thing again, police were summoned and made a search of the area.

Word soon spread that the Jersey Devil had invaded Gibbstown—in fact, *The Record* of November 22, 1951, sported just such a headline: "JERSEY DEVIL 'INVADES' GIBBSTOWN." In the frenzy that followed, crowds of teenagers who roamed the town and the surrounding woods reported hearing "unearthly screams." Jerry Ray, one of the teens, claimed that it "almost grabbed" him, and he described the creature as having "a wild look in its eyes." And Ray was not the only one who claimed to have seen the Jersey Devil. Accounts were many and varied. Some said it was seven feet tall, its face ugly. One person claimed with excitement that it was half-human, half-animal; others depicted this strange invader as a chunky man with a bestial face. Chief of Police Louis Sylvestro had his hands full with this commotion. He had to follow up on the rash of reported sightings while his office staff handled countless phone calls. To make matters worse, carloads of curiosity seekers, hoping for a glimpse of the Jersey Devil, were jamming the quiet streets of the town. The police posted signs saying, "The Jersey Devil is a Hoax," in a vain attempt to stem the flow of extra traffic. The students of the Gibbstown schools were so wrought up that principal Clarence Morgan summoned Chief Sylvestro to assist in calming the situation. In time, the Gibbstown incident faded, but the people who lived there during those hectic days still recall the turmoil.

Next, the Jersey Devil was reported prowling around Batsto and Upper Freehold Township in 1952, and in 1955, he was accused of attacking dogs in the vicinity of Jackson Mills. In October 1957, foresters from the Parks and Forests Department found some burned, eerie remains at Hampton Furnace, a remote location in the Pines. The remains consisted of a partial skeleton, claws, feathers, bone particles, and the hind legs of some unrecognizable creature. Some thought this was nothing more than a hoax or old trophy, but others were relieved at the idea the Jersey Devil might finally have passed away.

Their relief was short lived, however, because the Jersey Devil was

The mansion at Batsto, Wharton State Forest. According to tradition, Batsto is one of the Jersey Devil's favorite haunts. Photography by Susan Miller

not dead. In Dorothy, near Mays Landing, piercing cries and unidentified tracks caused a stir in 1960. Officials proclaimed that these phenomena were caused by owls, hawks, and large rabbits, but many people slept with guns to defend themselves from what they saw as much more threatening than these official explanations. Game Warden Joseph Gallo and State Game Trapper Carlton Adams set traps throughout the area and remained on alert.

Early one evening around 1961, Charles Romano and Joe Hartman went bow-and-arrow hunting for deer off Jackson Road, near Indian Mills. Romano had a deer call, but Hartman told him not to use it in this area, because he thought it might spook the deer instead of attracting them. Romano climbed into a deer stand while Hartman went off to hunt on foot. Romano still remembers very vividly what happened next: "A short time later, I spotted something coming up a rise to my right, walking across me from right to left. There was still plenty of light and the woods in this area was more like Pennsylvania than New Jersey—there was little underbrush and the grass was only about six inches high. Upon reaching the top of the rise, I began hearing a sound, not a movement sound but a sound from whatever it was. One hundred or so feet away, I thought about shooting it, that's how sure I was that it wasn't human. My thinking was, I would be famous if I hit it, but not being a very good shot, my fear prevented me from shooting. I was breathing hard and shaking."

As his fear mounted, Romano noted the details of the monster: "My first thought was [that it was] an animal escaped from a circus. It had reddish hair all over; I didn't notice a tail or any facial features. It walked upright, not bent over and had short quick steps, making a sound all the while. I watched it, trying not to make my presence known. It was about five feet tall, a few inches one way or another; after losing sight of it, I climbed out of the stand and walked fast back to the car."

Hartman did not see the creature but had heard strange sounds, which he thought had been Romano using the deer call.

One very cold day in December 1965, Robert Nisky, Jr. and a relative visited a house in Leeds Point, which is considered by many people to be the Jersey Devil's birthplace. After looking around the house and surrounding grounds, they headed back to the car, and, as he told the authors, "all of a sudden we heard a super-loud scream—I mean loud—coming from the upstairs of the house. May God strike me, this is the truth, all true." Nisky and his relative rapidly left the area.

In the late 1960s, the Green Bank and Lower Bank areas were plagued by a series of mysterious screams. Barry Cavileer, of Lower Bank, reported that in 1965, many area residents heard awful noises emanating from the woods on the road from Green Bank to Weekstown. These cries persisted over a period of several days. A Lower Bank man attempted to determine the origin of the screams, and bravely plunged into the woods along the Mullica, but as he neared the source of the sounds, a large bird suddenly soared out of the trees and flew across the river.

One day in July 1968, a pickup truck with a group of campers was passing a blueberry field near Bell Haven Lake. Over the normal rattle of the truck on the summer road, they heard a sound described by Dave Martino, later a ranger with the Parks and Forests Department, as "a high-pitched, cracking scream," with a definitely recurring pattern. A few of the cries were muffled, as if intermittently choked off. After the driver stopped the truck, the campers observed something thrashing about in the blueberry bushes, but even though it was broad daylight, they could make out only a dark outline.

Bill Kronmaier, who for 23 years owned the Sweetwater Casino, a popular restaurant along the Mullica, thinks he saw the Jersey Devil. An avid fisherman, Kronmaier was driving to a tournament in Atlantic City between 3:30 and 4:00 A.M. one morning in June 1969. As he passed through Weekstown, the glare of his headlights clearly caught a large animal with long, slender legs, somewhat like those of a goat or a deer. As Kronmaier watched in amazement, the tailless creature sprinted across the road. The stunned Kronmaier knew immediately what he had seen. He informed the authors, "I always swear it was the Jersey Devil. I don't know, some people laugh, but I swear."

On a late fall day in 1974, Howard Mosley, of Whiting, was sitting in his Barnegat Sneakbox (a small boat unique to the area) on Reed's Bay, off Brigantine. It was dawn, and Mosley was scanning the area in search of ducks when he spied a strange-looking, furry animal on the shore about 200 yards away. "I'm not believing what I'm seeing," Mosley told himself as he blinked to clear his vision, but the "thing," with a kangaroo-like lower body and an upper torso tapering into a form reminiscent of a goat, was still there, perched on its hind legs. As the astounded Mosley watched, the creature (which Mosley later described to the authors as tailless and weighing about 90 pounds) gave a loud snort and hopped off into the vegetation.

Sometime during August 1975, in Williamstown, New Jersey, a horse was found with its throat torn out. Some ascribed this to the work of the Jersey Devil. The following summer, a service station attendant from Jackson Mills was in a panic when for several nights in a row the Jersey Devil followed him home by tracking him through the woods beside the road. Alarmed by this shadowing, the man began carrying a gun, which seemed to scare the Jersey Devil, who ceased following his prey.

In November 1976, a number of pigs were found dead in the Pedricktown vicinity. Some of these deaths could be attributed to cholera. On the other hand, the cause of death of many of them could not be determined, and other pigs had been mutilated. At least one had been carried off by something unknown, and its blood left a trail along some bushes at a height of some three feet off the ground. The Jersey Devil was widely blamed for these unexplained deaths.

At this time in the nearby Carneys Point area, Ray Smallwood observed the mayhem taking place among some local livestock. Several 110- to 115-pound pigs, not fully grown, appeared to have been lifted out of their pen and dragged 500 yards. Their throats were eaten out, and claw marks scored their backs and shoulders. Mysterious footprints were found in the area. In addition to Smallwood, the people on whose farm the mutilations took place were witnesses. After the wife saw a big creature with a long tail run across the road, she carried a gun when she worked on the farm.

Even the deer population in this area temporarily declined.

The summer of 1977 was an active period for the Jersey Devil. After he made an appearance in Chatsworth, the Devil surprised a South Jersey woman while she was picking blueberries. When she observed the frightening creature eating blueberries by the boxful, she fled, leaving her fresh-picked berries behind. In another incident, a large, hairy beast grabbed the door handle of a woman's car in Penns Grove, and the distraught woman claimed the creature was able to run alongside

the car at speeds of up to 60 miles per hour. Around this time, a number of campers in the Tuckerton vicinity were awakened one night by a strange chopping sound, which went on for supernaturally long periods of time. No sooner had the chopping ceased than a loud crash was heard from the vicinity of the trailer in which a number of the campers were housed. Afraid of whatever was out there, the campers waited, full of anxiety, until morning to investigate. They found a dent in the side of the trailer, and round prints driven up to two inches into the soil in several spots, and running under the trailer, which had only a foot-high clearance. The prints went off into the woods.

The Jersey Devil ushered out the 1970s by making several unwelcome visits. In October 1979, the *Wall Street Journal* reported a Jersey Devil sighting on January 16, 1978. Dale English, a Chatsworth teenager, was ice skating with a friend when they detected a repulsive odor, "like a dead fish," permeating the area. Soon, they saw "two big red eyes staring at us" and a creature who "was about seven feet tall." They ran to summon their families, but by the time they returned, snow had obliterated any traces of the monster.

In June 1978, two women who were experienced in the nature and history of the Pine Barrens were camped illegally along the abandoned railroad tracks in Atsion, but the Jersey Devil was to shorten their unregistered stay. As a state forest ranger later told the authors, the women were awakened by unearthly screams and violent thrashing around in the bushes outside their tent. They sent their large dog out to investigate, but the animal rapidly retreated back into their tent. The two campers finally fled to the safety of an all-night diner in Hammonton.

Also, during this period, real estate agents had trouble selling or even leasing a house south of Manahawkin along Route 9. Several prospective buyers and renters backed out of deals after seeing a large, red monster with bat-like wings and an alligator-like tail.

The 1980s began with a fresh rash of Jersey Devil incidents. He was seen by unnamed witnesses, running across the road in New Egypt early in 1980. During the winter of 1980–81, the Jersey Devil was busy banging on sheds, turning over trash cans, and frightening people and pets around the Waretown vicinity.

The summer of 1981 saw at least two Jersey Devil incidents. In June, a group of people were canoeing along the Mullica, close to shore, as some mysterious beast kept pace with them through the underbrush near the water. The following month, a group of young women in their early twenties had a reunion with a camping trip in the Pines just outside of Waretown. They claim they spent a night of terror as the Jersey Devil thrashed around in the woods outside their tents, peering in at them with bright red eyes.

The Devil Gets into Politics

It all started in the spring of 1981, with an article that appeared in the *National Examiner,* a Canadian newspaper, entitled "Revealed: Demon Roams New Jersey Coast." The ruckus was based on an interview with Floyd West, mayor of Bass River Township and a member of the Pinelands Commission. In its March 24, 1981, issue, the *Examiner* said that according to Floyd West, "The loathsome fiend actually breeds with local women, who then give birth to half human-half demon children." West, according to the article, continued, "Women who have carnal knowledge of the Jersey Devil produced monstrous, evil children." The article went on to attribute these further quotes to West: "The Jersey Devil is definitely a supernatural being who takes the forms of animals and people. It's not an entertaining matter. . . .People from the outside consider him just a legend. But the folks who live here know he's real and know his character. . . .Encounters with the demon leave people crippled with fear." The previous October, NEA, a wire service, carried an article entitled "Jersey Devil Is Back to Haunt Us," written by Tom Tiede, in which West is quoted as saying, "It's true, the Jersey Devil is still here. Sometimes people hear it thrashing about in the darkness. Sometimes people come face to face with it. I know it sounds preposterous, but anyone who stays out very long in the Pine Barrens is going to believe."

After the Canadian newspaper article circulated in Bass River Township, angry citizens demanded Mayor West's resignation and posted signs along Route 9 to voice their indignation. One sign read, "Welcome to Demonsville, Land of Satanic Pleasure (Devil Made Us Do it!)." Another proclaimed, "Development for Sale, Jersey Devil Reality [*sic*], Flo-Wes Broker." The signs, placed by Ken Hayek, Gary Piper, and Bob Mitchell, were torn down, but one undamaged sign was rescued and reset on a private lawn.

Soon a petition for the recall of Mayor West was circulating. In response, West told the *Sunday Press* of Atlantic City, "I feel like Carol

Burnett [Carol Burnett successfully sued a tabloid for misrepresenta-
tion]. . .At first I thought it was some kind of a joke. I didn't think people believed what they read in those rags." West called the *Examiner* article "pure fabrication," and asserted, "I never gave the *Examiner* an interview. I had no contact with them at all. I don't even buy any of
those newspapers. The whole thing is made up of thin air." West announced his intentions, later, to sue the *National Examiner* if it had U.S.
holdings.

Bass River Township had been experiencing local political controversy, over the question of land development in the Pines, sewer im-
provements, and the like, before the Jersey Devil controversy. Some of
the citizens expressed their indignation with the Jersey Devil article in
a written statement, in which they called the article "the straw that
broke the camel's back." Like a summer storm in the Pines, the controversy eventually passed with time. But it is interesting to note the Jersey Devil has been part of a contemporary political controversy.

Some Recent Sightings: The Jersey Devil Still Out There

Randy and Barbara Higgenbottom, of Paisley, recounted to the authors
some interesting experiences in the early 1980s. In 1983, they heard
terrible cries coming from the woods. Barbara said, "It sounded like a
woman screaming." In 1984, this eerie screaming proved so loud that
woodcutters heard it over the sound of their chainsaws—they ended
up fleeing the woods.

A woman living in Winslow Township, Camden County, claims to
have had recurring Jersey Devil experiences over the years. One time,
she saw it breaking off small trees on her property, but the creature was
too far away for her to get a good look. In the fall, she has often heard
heavy breathing outside of her house. The latest incident of this type
was in 1993.

In late 1995, there were two separate, very interesting reports. As
she told the authors, Sue Dupre was driving in the vicinity of Pompton
Lakes on Route 287 when a strange creature rocketed across the lanes
of the expressway. She thought a car might have grazed it, but it appeared unharmed as it moved with nearly supernatural speed. Sue

caught a glimpse of an armadillo-like face, and she observed that the creature moved in a hopping motion like a kangaroo. Also that year, Michael Dorofee, of New Gretna, noticed an unusual light moving around the tops of the pines near his home at night. He was not sure what it was, but added that "strange things happen in the land of the Jersey Devil."

That sentiment is shared by many people.

IV

JERSEYITES TELL THEIR TALES: COLLECTORS AND MORE WITNESSES SPEAK

The Jersey Devil is a familiar part of New Jersey culture. Some have grown up hearing of this famous South Jersey demon's exploits, and others have actively pursued the lore of the Jersey Devil, coming up with interesting bits of information in the process. And, of course, there are those who have had the transfixing experience of encountering a weird denizen of the Pine Barrens.

Henry Charlton Beck and Early Witness Memories

Henry Charlton Beck, through his well-read collection of tales written in the 1930s, brought about widespread recognition of the Pine Barrens and its famous monster. Beck's collection of tales recounts contemporary beliefs of the Jersey Devil and, as with folklore, tales that go far back into the origins of the legend. Herbert Halpert's folklore studies during the 1940s increased scholarly attention to the area and the Jersey Devil. But then, a few journalists made it fashionable to cast aspersions on the people of the Pine Barrens and their way of life. Consequently, many residents of the Pine Barrens became reluctant to talk with outside researchers. As time passed and worldwide interest in the supernatural escalated, however, some people relaxed their protective silence and started talking about the Jersey Devil again.

One of the first things older residents relate is that they feared the Jersey Devil while growing up. Walter Edge, twice governor of New Jersey, United States senator, and ambassador to France, noted, "When I was a boy down in Atlantic County. . . we were threatened with the Jersey Devil, morning, noon, and night." Edge's memory reflects that of many. Geraldine Witt, of Penns Grove, says, "I remember the Jersey Devil when I was thirteen years old, and that was our mother's way of getting us kids to come home after dark. The Jersey Devil had two hooves like a cow and was built like a man. It was very tall, naked, and full of long hair. We were pretty scared of the Jersey Devil in the late 1920s."

Ann and Winslow Waters, of Swedesboro, remember parents often scared children into behaving just by mentioning the Jersey Devil, and writer William Kunze recalls that children were told no place but the outhouse was safe from the Devil's revenge. The Jersey Devil could even slip through keyholes! This threat worked well, making children afraid to misbehave. Exploiting this fear, a few Delaware Township (now Cherry Hill Township) farmers painted footprints on the sides and roofs of their barns and proclaimed them to be the work of the Jersey Devil. This practice tended to keep mischievous children away.

Elizabeth Harrison caught the Jersey Devil hysteria and developed a fear of a stained glass window on the stair landing of her house. It contained a figure that looked "so much like the Jersey Devil's description" that she would not go past it alone but would sit on the bottom steps and scream until an older brother or sister escorted her past the terrifying sight.

Al Edwards, of Beach Haven, reported to the authors that he vividly remembers "riding from Florence, N.J. to the shore in a rumble seat of my brother's car (a Chevy Runabout) after dark. . . to Long Beach Island through the pines on the old narrow dirt road, and being half scared to death looking on both sides of the road 'cause we heard the J.D. could run as fast as the car. So you can imagine how we felt sitting out in the open going through the Jersey Pines."

Even in the 1960s, many grade school children still believed strongly in the Jersey Devil. Mary Ann Thompson, a Vincentown cran-

berry grower, recalls that belief in the Jersey Devil was strong: he was looked upon as a friendly sort, but nevertheless no one was eager to encounter him. Her father told her the story of people seeing the Jersey Devil coming out of the chimney of Vincent Leeds' house (the place was named after him). Mary's father also recalled the Devil was a popular figure of fear along the Rancocas Creek, and canoe parties always tried to hurry past the Mill Street Bridge in Vincentown, since the place was rumored to be one of his favorite haunts. Ms. Thompson also recalls that in the mid-1960s, at Red Lion, a couple ran their car off the road after they spotted the Jersey Devil.

Daniel Leeds Mathews

Daniel Leeds Mathews, Jr., still called himself "Junior" although he was of advanced age when he met the authors. Mr. Mathews was born in Oceanville, near Leeds Point, in 1894. The son of an oysterman,

Mathews was one of the oldest living former residents of Galloway Township and was related to several old families in the region, such as Mathews-Mathis, Leeds, Sooy, and Somers. Mathews remembered that the Jersey Devil was often a topic of discussion at the gatherings that followed family funerals. The mourners swapped chilling tales of the bloodcurdling cries heard in the woods over the years. Mathews' aunt, Delphine Somers, who claimed she had heard the Devil, told him, "If you ever heard it, you'd never forget it."

Mathews also shared a story his father had told him. It seems that two older relatives from the Somers family had a run-in with the Jersey Devil in the 1890s. One night, the two men (a father and a son) took up a position in the woods off Somerstown Lane, near Oceanville. They cocked their guns and lay in wait for the Jersey Devil. Then, they heard it crashing noisily through the woods behind them. The sound grew louder and louder before the Devil briefly and frighteningly came into sight—dashed by them in the moonlight, and ran off. The two men were so shaken they were unable to shoot, and they ran full speed down the lane to the safety of their house.

Earl Danley

Renard Wiseman, of New Gretna, and Earl Danley, of Burlington, a New Jersey forest ranger, concur that legend indicates that the Jersey Devil is most likely to appear during the full moon. He also seems to have a fondness for Halloween. The Devil was believed by many people in the Jobstown-Wrightstown section of Burlington County to be a vegetarian. Because of this, campers used to leave shoes outside of their tents at night so that the Jersey Devil would realize that beings, and not plants, were inside the tents. (Of course, if the Devil were a vegetarian, that would absolve him of blame in the animal mutilations for which he has been credited.)

Danley remembers many rich tales of the creature, told to him by his older relatives. Most of these took place in the Jobstown-Wrightstown area in the 1920s, before the advent of the sprawling Fort Dix complex.

Danley's kin told him that three or four men from the area would periodically go on a "Jersey Devil hunt." Though they were equipped with lanterns and shotguns, the hunters always fled after hearing strange, eerie noises emanating from the forest depths.

Another of Danley's family tales involves an attempt to shoot the Devil. One night, a farmer heard strange sounds in his barnyard. Seizing his shotgun and a lantern, he dashed out the door in time to see something dark running alongside his barn. The farmer blasted the creature with a shotgun, and in the morning, he found the seven-foot-tall silhouette of the Jersey Devil on the side of the barn—precisely shaped by the shotgun pellets that he had sprayed around the creature's body. The silhouette perfectly matched the local description of the monster: a kangaroo shape, a deer head, short front feet, long back feet, and wings. It was also believed that the prints left by the Jersey Devil resembled those of a deer, and that it had a bushy porcupine tail with long end needles which acted as an effective deterrent against any foolhardy individual who might attempt to seize the beast by its tail.

Alex Platt

There are many collectors of Jersey Devil information, a number of whom are important sources of data.

One of these investigators, Alex Platt, of Jackson Township, a public accountant and historian, has been collecting Jersey Devil tales for over twenty years. Genial and gregarious, Mr. Platt has the knack for getting along with a variety of people, creating an atmosphere in which they can talk freely. During his years in the Jackson area, he has become acquainted with numerous residents and heard much of its history and lore.

One of the most vivid accounts Platt has come across is from a Whitesville couple, who had a shocking encounter with Jersey's famous demon in 1953. One evening around dusk, the wife stormed out of the house after an argument with her husband. As she sat in their car to cool off, she heard the door being rattled, and she turned to see a weird creature trying to get in the car with her. The woman screamed in terror, quickly locking all the doors. Hearing her cries, her husband charged out of the house with a gun. But before he could get off a shot, the creature, with a limping type of step, ran off into the woods, waving its webbed hands. The distraught couple described the thing as black, with short, seal-like fur, webbed hands and feet, large glowing eyes, and standing about four and a half feet tall. It seemed to move about in a crouched position.

Platt also has talked to a prominent businessman who, in 1956, was an egg-truck driver on a route that took him from Ocean County to Vineland daily, stopping at the farms along the way. Very early one morning, as he slowed the truck to stop for an egg pickup near New Gretna, the headlights illuminated a stream from which a six-foot, hairy Jersey Devil was rising. It ran on two feet, placing its front paws briefly on the hood of the truck. The creature then ascended a nearby ridge, using its front paws to accelerate its climb.

Another tale told to Platt concerns a woman who in 1960, when she was 25, had the fright of her life near what is now Great Adventure Park. As she drove from Freehold to Jackson, where County Routes 537 and 571 intersect, the woman saw a little, man-like creature who sat on his haunches in the middle of the road, flapping his wings. He moved aside just enough to let the car pass, as he beat his wings in a violently threatening manner. The shaken woman sped from the area.

One of the most harrowing tales Platt has heard occurred in 1975, to a young man who was driving home late one night along Fischer Boulevard in Toms River. As he cruised along, a six-foot, hairy creature jumped out in front of the young man's car. The young man was badly shaken, but having just passed a police car, he turned around and sped back to the policeman, who returned with him to the scene. The policeman, with some nonchalance, directed the young man to stay in the car while the officer went into the woods with a flashlight to investigate.

It was a short wait. Soon the officer ran from the woods in an obvious state of panic and jumped into the young man's car. Though the young man broke speed limits leaving the scene, there wasn't a murmur of complaint from his passenger. He suffered nightmares for many weeks after this incident, though he felt lucky to have escaped unscathed.

Platt also relates a story of something in the swampy thicket along Cook Road in Jackson that periodically disturbed the neighborhood dogs around 1973. A strange thrashing in the swampy water caused the frightened dogs to bark wildly. About this same time, an undetermined number of large dogs were mysteriously mauled at different locations between Waretown and Forked River. Strange footprints were found around many of the carcasses.

Mr. Platt asserts that most of the sightings he has come across have taken place in or near water, as if the Jersey Devil wanted to hide his trail.

A Prominent Anonymous South Jersey Witness

One prominent South Jersey citizen, who wishes to remain anonymous, was a helpful source of information about the Jersey Devil. From living in the Pine Barrens for a considerable time and meeting many residents and visitors, this man has gained a vast repertoire of stories about the creature.

He tells the experience of a long-time area resident, now dead, who encountered the Jersey Devil one afternoon during the 1920s. The boy and a friend were bicycling along what was little more than a narrow track through the Pinelands linking two small towns. As they pedaled along rapidly, they realized that *something* was keeping pace with them in the dense woods, at a distance of six to eight feet parallel to the road. It would have been difficult enough for anyone running on the road to keep up with the bicycles, but this *something* was running through thick woods and underbrush.

As they pedaled along, the young man and his friend caught glimpses of the creature. It was large and man-like, and its strange, loud breathing sent an eerie chill through them. The faster the terrified boys rode, the faster the Jersey Devil ran to keep abreast of them. The chase continued all the way to town. The frightened cyclists both stated, "It had to be the Jersey Devil!"

Many years later, the son of one of the cyclists was camping with his wife and three children in a New Jersey state forest. They heard a strange noise, and realized something was close to their tent, breathing so heavily it sounded like blasts of steam. The family felt a strong sense of fear, which our informant says is characteristic of any encounter with the Jersey Devil. Eventually, however, the creature retreated back into the woods.

A Medford woman told our prominent informant that she had had an encounter with the Jersey Devil in 1950, when she was around eleven years old. One night, she looked out her window and was astonished to see the Devil gazing in at her. She described the apparation as a "terrible-looking" thing, man-like but not a man, with a human form but clearly not human. Nor was it the common artist's conception of a devil. Somehow, she knew it had been looking in for some time, and it appeared to be in no hurry to leave. In terror, the girl screamed for her mother as the creature disappeared into the night.

Our informant himself felt the terror of a visitation from the Jersey Devil on the night of December 12, 1978, at about 1:00 A.M. He was driving from Chatsworth when the incident took place. The road was smooth and wide at this point, and he was alert and driving toward the center of the road as a precaution against hitting any deer that might dash suddenly from the woods. Yet to the man's surprise, a deer flew out of the air, at a supernaturally high arc, and dropped straight down onto the windshield and hood of his car. He fought to bring the car, which was travelling at 50 miles an hour, to a stop.

To this day the man believes that the deer was possessed by the Jersey Devil when it jumped 25 feet in the air. This prominent, respected citizen is convinced the Jersey Devil has the power to excite animals to do supernatural feats. In another instance in the late 1960s, a deer charged a long distance before crashing through the door of a Pinelands school. This anonymous gentleman refers to the Jersey Devil as "The Prince of the Pine Barrens" and he adds that the creature can possess people as well as animals. He believes the Jersey Devil is an evil spirit that has no form of its own but moves into the bodies of animals or humans. This may account for the many varied descriptions in the legend.

Our source also is certain that it is the Jersey Devil who creates an atmosphere of terror in the Pines. He says this is the common thread of Jersey Devil manifestations and has been so for centuries. He notes that the Native Americans passed quickly through the Pine Barrens on their way to summer fishing along the Jersey Shore. When settlers came from the British Isles, their native beliefs, rich in supernatural creatures, added to this dimension of the Pines.

This prominent informant believes the Jersey Devil is unquestionably real. "If you spend time out there, you are going to be bumping into him," he warns. "The Jersey Devil is in charge of the Pine Barrens. He has power and influence there."

William Kunze

A personal brush with the Jersey Devil helped spark William Kunze's interest in this famous demon. Kunze was raised on a farm in Deer Park, along Old Marlton Pike in Delaware Township (now Cherry Hill Township), where this incident also occurred. One cool night in November 1917, as Kunze was walking rapidly to the outhouse, he had an experience with this creature he was never to forget. There, near the building, sat a brown creature, several feet tall, with two small hornlike objects protruding from its head, and with glowing yellow eyes! He fled from the creature. Though the outhouse might have been considered safe from the Jersey Devil, according to lore, the creature here had blocked his path. Kunze remembered well, "I was never so scared in my life. To me, there was no doubt that this was the Jersey Devil."

For more than sixty years, William Kunze lived at Ship Bottom, on Long Beach Island. In years past, Kunze found true concern about Jersey Devil visits in the Shore area. Between the infamous Jersey mosquitoes and the belief in the Jersey Devil, people tended to stay indoors at night. In the 1930s and '40s, concern about the Jersey Devil began to wane, as Kunze recalled. But in more recent years, he saw a rekindling of interest in the creature and the lore that surrounds it. The resurgence of interest in the Jersey Devil has resulted in the proliferation of Jersey Devil t-shirts, writings, folklore, and popular history.

Kunze considered today's concerns with preservation of the environment would create an expanded wildlife population, and this increase will result in more animal sightings, some of which are bound to be reported as Jersey Devil incidents.

Tom Brown, Jr.

Tom Brown, Jr., in his autobiographical best-selling book, *The Tracker*, details his encounter as a twelve-year-old with the Jersey Devil. While undergoing wilderness survival training alone in the Pine Barrens, he had a most frightening experience. "I could hear it coming through the brush toward me, snapping branches out of its way as if it hated everything it came in contact with. I was frozen with terror and then I started jumping around and waving my knife at it to ward it off. I saw it only as a huge dark shadow coming out of the trees with a ghostly white luminescence around it. I *knew* it was the Jersey Devil." Brown's fear turned to rage as he swung his knife at the huge apparition, which retreated as Brown pursued it for 200 yards or so, before he fell down in exhaustion. Upon reflection over the years, Brown has concluded that his fear of the Jersey Devil may have influenced his thinking and that, in fact, it might have been some other hapless animal he encountered that day.

Jack Wiseman

Jack Wiseman, of New Gretna, retired Superintendent of the Burlington County Mosquito Commission, father of Renard Wiseman and cousin of Herb Mathis, has many Jersey Devil tales to tell.

As a young boy, Wiseman often heard his relatives speak of the Jersey Devil. His uncle, Jeff Cranmer, for example, would go fishing for perch in the fall, but he always made sure he was home before dark: Cranmer warned his nephew that fall nights were especially likely times for the Jersey Devil to appear.

Wiseman had his own frightening experience with the Jersey Devil during July 1924, in the New Gretna area.

> My uncles John and Fred took me fishing down to Dove's Point, where we caught a lot of perch. It was getting late when we left the meadows, and by the time we started through the woods on Phillip's Road it was getting dark. This road is about one mile long, and at that time ran through a dense wooded area (now it is built up and the Parkway goes through it).
>
> We had been walking down Phillip's Road for about five minutes when we heard this terrible scream. It began to get closer as we travelled down the road. Uncle John told Uncle Fred to take me by the hand and run, which he did. Uncle John stayed back with the fish, and would throw a fish every now and then. We ran out of fish about two-thirds of the way through the woods. Both uncles took my hands and practically carried me the rest of the way to my Uncle Merrill's house. He had a dairy farm at the

end of the road. You could hear the noise going through the woods until it got to Stony Swamp, then it stopped. Both my Aunt Ada and Uncle Merrill were out listening to it when we came up to the house. Aunt Ada said that "we heard the noise sitting on the porch and knew you would be coming through the woods soon." The following morning, about 4:00 A.M., when Uncle Merrill went out to feed and milk the cows, there were no cows in the barn. They were all in the upper pasture. As he entered the barn to get the cows, It made a loud screech, and knocked him down, spilling the contents of the buckets. Uncle Merrill said It was "a big brown thing, with a large head, and bigger than a police dog." The cows wouldn't come to the barn until it got daylight.

Sometime around this period, Wiseman said, Josh Mathis, a relative, was visited by a mysterious intruder as well. Mathis was sitting on his porch rocker one moonlit night when something light brown and about six feet tall dashed around the corner of his house. The thing ran through the tomato patch, tearing up some plants before disappearing into the woods.

In November 1950, Jack Wiseman was helping Russell and Florence Smalley build a house. Suddenly, they heard a noise and Wiseman pointed a floodlight in the direction from which it came. Something with glowing orange eyes was hopping about at the edge of the woods. When the light struck it, the creature began screeching and ran deep into the forest. According to Wiseman, the Smalleys and Wiseman agreed there would be no more night work.

In the 1970s, Wiseman continued to have strange encounters with this phenomenon from the Pines. In the winter of 1972, he found tracks that seemed to have no clear ending or beginning, around the periphery of his property. In August 1978, Wiseman heard a strange noise just as he saw his cat running away from something. Taking a closer look, he saw two eyes which seemed to be disembodied. As the eyes moved through his barn, Wiseman shot in their direction—in vain. A tank on the property still bears witness to the dent of one of the shots.

On several occasions near Martha Furnace and south of Lake Oswego, Wiseman also has observed some strange markings in the sand. It appeared that some unusual creature with strange footprints had been digging and rolling in the sand and tearing up nearby bushes.

Belva Browne and Bessie Carr LoSasso

Two elderly South Jersey residents are strong examples of people who have openly acknowledged their experiences with the Jersey Devil. Belva Browne, of Barnegat, and Bessie Carr LoSasso, of Nesco, both have had frightening first-hand encounters.

Belva Browne, who was born in 1895 in Barnegat and lived her entire life there, recalled vividly the night in 1905 her mother, her sister, and she saw the Jersey Devil. The three were returning home around 8:00 P.M. on a cold winter night. As they walked through the newly fallen, light snow along the garden path, they could see by the full moon the bean poles her father had leaned against a sour cherry tree for winter. Suddenly the trio spied the Jersey Devil circling the tree. It had a large, bulky body, a slender head, and pointed ears. "Mom, there's that thing," cried Belva, as they all started to run. When they ran through the front door of the house, their Boston Terrier was hiding under the couch. Belva Browne recalled, "I saw it and I know what I've seen. I saw the Jersey Devil. That's no lie, it's authentic."

Within a few minutes of the Brownes' encounter with the creature, Mrs. Wilson, a local teacher, observed the Jersey Devil "swooping over the tree tops" in back of her house. The next day several residents found footprints in the snow, including ones on the Brownes' porch roof. Rolf Collins, Barnegat's postmaster, made plaster casts of the prints, which reportedly are still in his daughter's possession.

Bessie Carr LoSasso was born three miles north of Chatsworth, and was one of thirteen surviving children. Bessie's father supported the family on as little as $1.25 a week that he earned by picking blueberries, gathering sphagnum moss, and cutting wood.

One day in 1914, Bessie, Mary Carr, and six other children were playing in the woods. It was about 1:00 P.M. when a deaf-mute child suddenly pointed into the forest. As the other children looked through the trees, an ugly, threatening creature emerged and walked to within four feet of the children. The creature stood on his hind feet, which were each a foot long. His forepaws were short, with hooked hands, and he held them limply in front of his chest, similar to a kangaroo. Bessie described the Jersey Devil as about four and a half feet tall, furry, with a long and ratlike tail, a grotesque face with a flattened nose like a pig, and two large horns sprouting from the top of his head. To add to his eerie, supernatural quality, the Devil was dragging chains, which clashed as he moved.

Years later, while driving in the vicinity of Chatsworth, the mother of one of the children saw a creature who precisely fitted the description provided by her frightened daughter years before.

Billy Dunnkosky

Billy Dunnkosky, of Howell Township, Monmouth County, performed folk and country and western music at Albert Hall, Waretown, New Jersey, Saturday nights, under the stage name of "Billy Dunn." Mr. Dunnkosky had at least half a dozen encounters with the Jersey Devil over the period of 1968–70. At the time, Dunnkosky was living along Route 9, seven miles south of Freehold. Until October 1970, these incidents consisted of hearing strange sounds like something prowling in the yard, but then the situation grew more serious.

For two or three nights running, something strange was visiting Billy Dunnkosky's yard. He tried to track it with several German Shepherds, but the big dogs put their tails between their legs and refused to cooperate. A frustrated Dunnkosky took a spotlight from the front of his house, and, shining the light around, he finally caught the Jersey Devil in the beams. The creature was "funny-looking, like a gorilla with big teeth. It was at least six feet tall and covered with hair." Dunnkosky, who claimed he was a good shot, "shot at it with a .22, but nothing happened!" Dunnkosky's brother strung barbed wire on a path they thought the monster would be using. In the daylight, the brothers found the barbed wire "broken up like straw" and footprints resembling human feet, but with only three toes. Dunnkosky summed it up by saying, "I'm pretty sure it was the Jersey Devil. That's what I say."

Other Memories and Tales

From the past to the present, the Jersey Devil has added a colorful dimension to the lives of many Jerseyites. Florence Moore, of Vincentown, recalls stories of how the Jersey Devil added excitement to hayrides around 1950. The kids would look off into the dark woods and see things that they imagined to be the creature.

The Jersey Devil even seemed to tap the local food supply. Many residents of the Pine Barrens believed that in the cold of winter, when milk bottles were left on the porch for too long, certain changes in the shape of the frozen cream indicated the Jersey Devil had been there. If frozen cream rising out of the bottle had deep indentations in the middle, that meant the Jersey Devil had been licking at it. If any eggs delivered to the door proved to be hollow, the Jersey Devil was blamed for sucking them dry.

Woodstown's Charles Haaf recalls stories that circulated during the Depression in the 1930s of a kinder Jersey Devil—turned Robin Hood—who left food on the doorsteps of families in need. Haaf also says that during this period, the thundering footsteps of the Jersey Devil were often heard crossing the bridge at Lower Bank during the wee hours of the night.

Jersey culture has many stories of encounters with the Pine Barrens' famous denizen. New Gretna's Gladys Wilson, proprietor of Pat's Stand and Union Hill Campground, retells her grandfather's story about a group who were crossing a bridge deep in the Pines when they encountered a monster, who charged them. One man grabbed a rail from the bridge and tried to finish off the creature, but the man finally conceded defeat by running away. In the late 1960s, at a spot in the Pines near New Gretna, horseback riders often reported that their animals had been spooked. A number of the riders spoke of an eerie feeling that something supernatural was lurking in the woods.

Tom Driscoll, of Tuckerton, remembered a strange incident that happened to him in 1923, when he was nine years old. He and his father were travelling along Western Avenue, near a swampy area. Suddenly, they heard something dashing through the woods and a hideous sound, "like somebody tearing a woman apart." Other people heard the sound too, and upon investigation, unusual prints were found in the area. An attempt was made to track the creature with dogs, but to no avail. Driscoll concluded that "the speed of that creature must have been very great, because he was making his way quickly through wet, swampy terrain." Of course, many involved believed they'd had a brush with the Jersey Devil.

Florence Moore knew someone who had her coat stolen by the Devil in 1940: As she walked home in the twilight along Richter Road, near Medford Farms, a dark, hairy thing darted out of the woods, seized her fur coat, and disappeared into the dark.

Alise Haley of Monmouth Beach says that "the Jersey Devil back in the 1800s was believed in by most. It was seen by reliable, stable, God-fearing folks." She remembers her grandfather, Tony Hulse, telling her of his two encounters with the creature. Hulse, who died in 1950 at the age of 96, lived in Osbornville, and it was there that he saw the Jersey Devil twice, around the 1870s.

The first time was on a dark night when he decided to take a ride on his horse. "He was peacefully trotting along the unlit road when a loud buzzing, whirling sound brought him to a halt," she says. "Above the pine trees he saw a blinding beam of light that slowly glided away far overhead. The powerful light was terrifying. Everyone agreed that it was that Devil again, up to his tricks."

The second sighting occurred during the summer, a few years after the first one. He was walking home from the local Baptist church following a heavy rain. Thinking he heard a galloping horse a short distance behind him, he moved to the side of the road. As the animal came into view, Hulse realized it was no ordinary horse. "This horse was ten times as large and breathing fire and smoke. My grandfather dashed for the closest tree, quickly climbing it to a branch out of danger. Very frightened, he waited until all was quiet again, glad that his home was not far off." Hulse returned to the site later and discovered large footprints in the muddy road. He shoveled one of them up with a wide board and put it on display in the general store in Osbornville.

And Herb Mathis, lifelong resident of New Gretna, remembers many unexplained activities occurring in that area, some of which may have been the work of the Jersey Devil. As a young boy in 1921, Mathis heard mysterious screams from the woods while out huckle-berrying with his family. One day, he was at his uncle Merrill Mathis' house while his uncle was butchering pigs. When weird screams came from the woods, his uncle sent him home.

Through many generations, the legend and the encounters persist. Weird cries, the unexplained and otherworldly appearance, strange encounters, all have been experienced by many generations of witnesses both in and around the New Jersey Pine Barrens.

V

BIGFOOT, OLD SALTS, AND DEVIL WORSHIP

As might be expected with a 250-year-old legend, the Jersey Devil is frequently associated with other monsters, folk traditions, and practices such as Satanism. In recent years, the famous Bigfoot has been spotted in New Jersey; consequently, comparison of these two famous monsters has become common. The Pine Barrens is so close to the sea that the lore of the Jersey Devil often has merged with maritime legends as well, and one of the most perplexing aspects of the Devil legend deals with the creature's relationship to witchcraft and devil worship.

Bigfoot

Bigfoot, sometimes called *Sasquatch* by the Native Americans of the western United States, has grayish-brown hair and sometimes sports a moustache and a beard. He stands seven to nine feet tall at maturity. He also has been reported to have an overpoweringly repulsive smell. Usually rather timid, he tries to get away as soon as possible whenever he encounters humans.

Bigfoot dates back to Native American times in the Northwest, but beginning in this century, Bigfoot sightings have been reported in New Jersey. While most of these Bigfoot sightings have been made in the mountains and swamps of northwestern New Jersey, a number have been reported in the southern part of the state as well—traditionally the home of the Jersey Devil. Some witnesses believe these appearances are not Bigfoot at all, but rather the more familiar Jersey Devil.

Robert E. Jones, of Byram Township, Sussex County, is the head of Vestigia, an organization that explores the unexplained, and he has researched Bigfoot sightings in New Jersey. Jones says there have been 92 eyewitnesses to Bigfoot appearances in the state, dating from 1910 to 1980. A number of sightings occurred in the 1970s.

Jones reports an unusual incident from around 1973, along the Jersey Shore. Hearing a scratching sound, an elderly woman looked out her window only to be confronted by a hideous face looking back at her. She screamed for her husband, and they both saw what they described as a Bigfoot creature in their yard. The woman felt sorry for the beast and began leaving food for it every night. One night, the couple heard a terrible crashing and looked out to see their garbage can flying through the air. It was then she realized she had forgotten to leave Bigfoot his nightly repast.

One of the more striking North Jersey sightings occurred in the spring of 1975, at High Point State Park, Sussex County. There, a former Green Beret, a veteran of the Vietnam War, was camping out. When a large, hairy, Bigfoot-like creature, thrashing around in the woods and emitting growls, screeches, and grunts, closed in on the isolated campsite, this usually fearless man fled. After investigating the incident, Jones emphasized, "This isn't a little old lady who got scared in the dark. He killed men in the jungles, and he wouldn't be frightened by a bear."

A few months later, Irving Raser and Charles Ames, of the New Jersey Division of Fish and Game, spotted something coming out of the fog in a Sussex County swamp. Rader explained, "Then I heard this noise. We got our eyes focused in on the swamp, and we saw this thing. We watched it, and we watched it, and didn't know what it was. Finally, I said, 'Charlie, that's Bigfoot.'"

Jay Adams, of Crandon Lake, says he has seen Bigfoot six times altogether. In fact, in April 1976 he saw what appeared to be a family of the creatures, five in all, in the Limecrest area of Sussex County. This particular group ranged in height from 4 1/2 feet to 15 feet, and left footprints as big as 24 inches.

The most harrowing Bigfoot sighting in North Jersey involved a Vantage family in May 1977 that was periodically frightened by the creature for one terrible week. It started one morning when the wife went to turn their dairy cows out to pasture. The animals were unwilling to move. As she prodded them, she heard a strange sound in the distance, which sounded "like a woman screaming while she was being killed." Puzzled by the sound, the woman walked around to the other side of the barn, to find a large wooden door ripped from its hinges. Looking around inside, she made a gruesome discovery. Six of their pet rabbits had been mutilated, their heads and legs torn from their bodies, and two of them seemed to have been crushed to death. Another two were missing. Surprisingly, however, there was little blood, and none of the victims appeared to have been used for food.

The next night, the family dog began a persistent, unremitting barking around 9:30 P.M. The woman and her 16-year-old daughter were quick to look out the window, and they saw a strange figure where the rabbits were kept. The husband, along with several friends and relatives who were visiting at the time, dashed outside to see "a big shadow—his head was as high as the eaves." When someone screamed, the thing took off into the apple orchard.

The family now braced for combat with Bigfoot. About the same time the next night, several members of the family, armed with guns, waited silently in the farmyard for the nocturnal raider. Once again, at about 9:30 P.M., the beast was spotted by the whitish light of a mercury vapor lamp used to illuminate the barnyard. The husband said, "At first all I saw were these two red eyes staring at me over there." The small posse opened a fusillade of fire at the beast, expending some thirty rounds from two rifles and two shotguns. The creature fled into an abandoned chicken coop and exited the other side, disappearing into the apple orchard.

The New Jersey State Police thought the whole episode was the work of a bear, but others had their doubts. Both Robert Jones, of Vestigia, and Marty Wolf, of the Society for the Investigation of the Unknown, followed up on the incident, and they concluded that it did not seem to be a bear. Jones believed the behavior was typical of Bigfoot: "I saw the dead rabbits. One had its head twisted off; that is a characteristic of Bigfoot." Wolf located several flat places in the grass, as though some large animal had been lying there.

Although many people involved in this case called the creature they encountered "Bigfoot," others argued that it was the Jersey Devil, moving into an area where he has not been frequently seen.

Legends of the Sea

As the Pine Barrens meet the salt marshes of the Jersey Shore, the folklore of both become intertwined. Many rich legends are made richer when combined with stories of the Jersey Devil.

No legendary figures of the sea are more fascinating than pirates, and no pirate evokes more interest than Captain Kidd. New Jersey's Barnegat Bay is only one of many places where the legendary Kidd supposedly buried treasure. The story goes that, sometime in the late seventeenth century, Kidd came ashore somewhere along this bay for one of these missions, and he had one of his crew beheaded so that the ghost would guard the treasure. This headless pirate reportedly became the companion of the Jersey Devil, and the two periodically were seen in the Pines and salt marshes. (In another, less common, version of the tale, the pirate still has his head.)

According to legend, the Jersey Devil often sat along Barnegat Bay, laughing when he saw sinking ships. It was even rumored that when he appeared along the shore, some poor ship was doomed to sink.

Many natural disasters have been blamed on the Jersey Devil. In January 1884, for example, when savage storms pounded the beaches

Although the Jersey Devil often appears in the Pine Barrens, salt marshes and bay sightings of the creature often occur. Ray Miller, photographer

of Atlantic City, some Jerseyites insisted the damaging squalls were the work of the Jersey Devil. Another storm-related legend warns that if you see a flying sheet, you should take cover because it is a sign the Devil is about to cause a ferocious storm.

One tale of the Jersey Devil's travels along Barnegat Bay involves his companionship with a large black dog. In much of folklore, black dogs are considered to be symbols of satanic forces, and this particular black dog blends pirate and satanic associations. The story tells of pirates who attacked and sunk a ship off Absecon Island, on which present-day Atlantic City is located. As the crew struggled to reach the shore, they were slaughtered by the merciless pirates. A young cabin boy and his pet black dog were among the victims. The spirit of this black dog made its way north from Absecon Island to Barnegat Bay, where it befriended the Jersey Devil. Many people claim to have seen the dog bounding along through the marshes by the side of the Jersey Devil.

The Golden Haired Girl is another companion of the Jersey Devil in his sojourns along the shore. This unfortunate wanderer, dressed in white, searches for her lover, who was lost at sea. The story goes that a beautiful girl from Manasquan was betrothed to a handsome ship's officer, but just before he left to make one last voyage before their wedding, the lovers quarreled bitterly. Realizing it would be a long time before she saw him again, the girl dashed to the dock to apologize, but she was too late. The mast of the ship was disappearing below the horizon. When the ship was due to return, the girl rushed down to the docks each day, gazing out to sea for a glimpse of the ship that would carry her lover back to her. Days, weeks, and months passed, all with no sign of the ship. But the lovely girl never gave up hope. Each day, she dressed in white, so her lover could see her as his ship crossed the horizon, and she went to the dock to await his arrival. The girl matured, became old, and finally died, but even death did not stop her vigil. The famous Golden Haired Girl in White still wanders the sands of the Jersey Coast, always looking eastward. Her only companion has been the Jersey Devil. Perhaps she finds some solace in this other lonely creature. According to legend, the beautiful Golden Haired Girl in White asks the people she meets if they have seen her loved one, and those who give a negative answer suffer 20 years of bad luck.

The Devil and Satanism

One of the more intriguing aspects of Jersey Devil lore raises the question of his legendary links with Devil beliefs, witchcraft, Satanism, and other negative occult subjects—including the mutilation of animals. Some say the Jersey Devil is an evil spirit who attracts bizarre cultists into remote sections of the Pine Barrens and marshes. Others are convinced that the vast undeveloped wilderness of this region attracts these people—not the Jersey Devil.

In the study of the Jersey Devil tradition, a few outside observers have, in essence, identified the Jersey Devil as being the same entity as the Devil, by calling traditional Devil lore tales of the *Jersey* Devil. To some degree, this is justified, as there is a kind of diabolic quality to the basic Jersey Devil tradition. After all, Mother Leeds' monstrous birth is usually attributed to a curse, and the Jersey Devil has been credited with many bad deeds.

Whether lured by tales of the Jersey Devil or by the cover of woods, it appears that some Satanists, cultists, or other practitioners of the negative paranormal periodically visit the area. One South Jersey official reports that incidents of devil worship in the Pine Barrens have increased in the last dozen years. This modern-day manifestation, he says, is due to the ongoing influence of the Jersey Devil. This official claims that "devil worshippers" from cities such as New York and Philadelphia are drawn to the Pine Barrens by the evil presence of the Jersey Devil spirit. Strange cries, screams, and chants can be heard emanating from deep in the Pines, especially during the full moons of warmer months. The devil worshippers this official and others describe come into the Pine Barrens in cars, vans, or on motorcycles, and practice quasi-Satanic rituals. Strange circles drawn in the sands of the Pines are a sign these mysterious ceremonies have been held there.

Over the years, many Jerseyites have reported witnessing groups dressed in long robes engaged in some sort of ceremony around a ritual fire deep in the woods. Are they innocently practicing some primitive form of worship, or are they communing with the Devil? Perhaps we will never know.

VI

CHASING THE JERSEY DEVIL

Part of the Jersey Devil phenomenon is the variety of ways people react to him—curiosity, terror, and aggression. The curious have sought to observe the creature. Many search groups have wandered South Jersey hoping for just a glimpse of this famous resident. The timid have fled in terror, and the aggressive have sought to capture, incapacitate, or even kill the Devil. A few have offered substantial rewards in the hope of deriving profits from displaying the captured monster. The history of the Jersey Devil is dotted with claims of his capture, injury, or death. Through the years, the police have often been called in to deal with this frightening creature.

Chases

During that famous week in January 1909, the Jersey Devil was pursued by a record number of searchers, as fear and curiosity blended in an attempt to come to grips with many widespread appearances. The *Philadelphia Public-Ledger* caught the spirit of the region during those days: "The hunt is on in nearly every town in South Jersey and unless the thing has a lair under the ground the hunters believe it is certain to be captured." Some of the posses formed during this emotionally charged period include one in Haddonfield, led by a Dr. Glover and a Mr. Holloway; another in Collingswood, headed by Station Agent Kirkwood; a posse in Westville, formed by Harry Doughten; and even Professor Marcus Farr of Princeton University led one through that part of the state. In the Riverton-Moorestown area, a posse of the "bravest young men" followed 20 bloodhounds through the snow as they sniffed out a trail of tracks. In Jacksonville, Burlington County, another posse attempted to have their dogs follow the trail, but the dogs were afraid and refused to do so. Burlington County farmers set out hundreds of baited steel traps. None of these measures succeeded.

Seven years later, a Jersey Devil sighting in the Clementon area so piqued the curiosity of a Philadelphia man that he led his family on a day-long excursion. Mrs. Mildred Shubert, then only a small child, remembers that summer day well. Her father loaded her, her mother, her five-year-old sister, and a picnic lunch into the family car and headed to the site, where they found several other people searching for the creature. Mrs. Shubert remembers vividly her father pushing the baby carriage with her sister inside, the wheels becoming stuck in the thin layer of sand covering the seemingly endless hills, while her mother tagged along behind, lugging the picnic lunch. They asked several people where the Jersey Devil might be found, but no one could give them a specific answer. Her mother finally convinced her father to give up the tedious search, and after the family ate their lunch, they returned home.

Another serious Jersey Devil search developed in the Bridgeport area during August 1927. The *New York Times* reported that a "Feathered Animal That Barks and Hoots" was being "hunted in New Jersey." On several occasions, residents out gathering huckleberries spotted what they said was the Jersey Devil. These encounters most often occurred in swampy locations. The witnesses described what they saw as being large and fast as a fox, but with feathers instead of fur. Its strange cry was a combination of a hoot and a bark. Instead of fleeing when they saw the Devil, one group of pickers tried to chase it, but the creaturet rapidly ran out of sight. Frank Rider, president of the local gun club, organized a posse, but their search was fruitless.

Other posses actively hunted the creature during the 1920s and 1930s. One group claimed they treed the Jersey Devil in Salem, and there was a report of a major posse operating in Pedricktown during the 1930s. Still another posse, following strange screams in the dark, scoured the woods and fields around Woodstown in 1936.

In July 1944, a number of people in Rancocas Woods, Burlington County encountered a thing they described as a black, hairy creature with a bad smell. It was soon rumored that the monster was the Jersey Devil. Police ordered people to stay away from Rancocas Creek, which seemed to be the creature's favorite haunt, but again, some residents roamed the woods and fields with guns. Two young brothers decided to take up the search, and each climbed a tree on opposite sides of a path. They had not been in their perches for very long when a foul-smelling creature dashed by them, giving them a terrible scare. A few weeks later, one of the brothers dashed into the house, exclaiming that someone had killed the creature. The brothers then rushed to the site, where they found a huge dead hog tied to a tree and a jubilant crowd milling around the carcass. One brother was satisfied this was the monster; however, to this day, the other brother insists the hog was not the dark, hairy creature that had run by them while they were hiding in the trees.

In October 1963, having studied the Jersey Devil, Nicholas DiMatteo, of Camden, drew a map of the Pines around Lake Atsion, which he had concluded would be a good location to search for the creature. Along with his friends Andrew Del Rossi and Martin Scarduzio, both of Camden; Berle Schwed, of Millville; and Glenn Emery, of Monroeville, DiMatteo plunged into the Pines. They hiked all morning, and then made camp in the thick forest near a lake. For some reason, DiMatteo's studies had led him to believe the Jersey Devil would appear in the area around this time.

Just after dark "The sounds started. . . and they seemed like a pack of wild dogs way out in the distance. . . . After about fifteen minutes the sounds came closer. They began to sound something like a big crowd at a football game," DiMatteo said. Schwed added, "It sounded more to me like wild screams—like cult worshippers or something." Not long before the noise began, the group had observed a series of strange footprints near where they were camped. The prints were 11 inches long and resembled those of a large bird, with the heel pressing deeper into the sand and the toes spread apart. The din continued to grow until it became a cacophony of frightening sounds, resembling the screams of a hundred people, mixed with long howls and strange metallic, chopping background noises. The shocked group waited until the sounds began to subside, and then rapidly worked their way through the dark forest back to the car. Emery concluded, "I know one thing, if any of us had tried to go after that thing he wouldn't be here today."

Recent efforts to find the Jersey Devil have met with as little success as past searches. According to William McMahon, in *Pine Barrens Legends, Lore, and Lies,* two Rutgers University students, armed with electronic search gear, tramped the woods for several nights in the vicinity of Leeds Point during the fall of 1974; their search was broken off when they were forced to leave under the incessant assault of Jersey mosquitoes. In October 1979, a few Stockton State College students claimed they saw the Jersey Devil in the fields and woods off Jimmy Leeds Road near campus. One night, a group of them conducted what they said was a thorough search of the area, but nothing was found. The Jersey Devil, if he had been there, had eluded searchers once again.

Alleged Jersey Devil Captures

On occasion, people claim to have actually captured the Jersey Devil. During January 1909, C.S. Hilk, a Trenton saloonkeeper, was told the Jersey Devil had been locked in a barn on a farm in Morrisville, Pennsylvania. Supposedly, the Devil had been simply sitting on a wagon as it was driven into the barn, and he was trapped inside when the barn door closed. Once they heard about the supposed capture, Hilk and several others rowed across the Delaware River the next day, but though they searched the barn thoroughly, they did not find a trace of the creature.

About the same time, rumors began circulating that the Jersey Devil had been captured and was being detained in a cell in Trenton's Second District police station. Veteran police buffs observed that one section of cells was being given inordinate security, and a few other unusual events also fueled the rumors. Clerk Hulm and Judge Rees finished their day's business rapidly and left, and far fewer people than usual were observed entering the building. The district's Captain Dettmar and Sergeant Schanck would neither confirm nor deny that the Jersey Devil was under arrest.

As news of the Devil's incarceration spread, hundreds of people crowded the street in front of the station and called for the Jersey Devil to be brought out on display. One woman even asked the police if they could bring a feather from the Jersey Devil's wing so she could put it in her hat as a souvenir. The curious clearly showed they were eager to see the famous monster, but their fear was evident. None of them seemed inclined to venture inside.

When he heard of the Devil's incarceration, Harry F. Smith, Superintendent of Cadwalader Park, requested permission to send a wagon to pick up the Jersey Devil for display in his park. Apparently not all Trentonians were convinced the Jersey Devil was imprisoned at the Second District police station. Throughout this episode, Sergeants Schanck and Culliton did not have a minute to spare. The telephone rang constantly with reports of Devil sightings. The incident at the police station came to a gradual end, as the crowds began to disperse, because another rumor had spread that the famous captive would not be displayed until morning.

Excited by the furor in the vicinity of his town during that famous week in 1909, Mayor Gable of Bordentown proposed a unique solution to the problem of the Jersey Devil. The mayor claimed to have footprints by the Devil "preserved in alcohol." He said he was saving them to try them on the Devil once it was captured, and that he was preparing a special padded cell in the town jail. To lure the beast into town, Mayor Gable said that he was putting "trained" watermelons, oranges, and grapes all over his yard.

The most infamous "capture" of the Jersey Devil was the work of the renowned hoaxter and showman Norman Jefferies, a publicist for T.F. Hopkins' 9th and Arch Museum in Philadelphia. Sensing the widespread Jersey Devil interest throughout the Delaware Valley, Jefferies announced with much fanfare that the Jersey Devil had been captured "following a terrific struggle." To ensure the safety of spectators, Jefferies displayed his "Leeds Devil, the fearful, frightening, ferocious monster which has been terrorizing two states" in "a massive steel cage." Jefferies cautioned the public, "Don't miss the sight of a lifetime." And the crowds came. For ten cents, they were treated to the Jersey Devil, a curio hall, and a vaudeville show. The cage was strewn with bones, and a young boy hidden in the back poked the poor creature with a stick to make it jump. Years later, Jefferies admitted that his "Jersey Devil" was a rented kangaroo from Buffalo, New York, which he painted green and outfitted with rabbit fur–covered wings.

Claims of Killing or Injuring the Jersey Devil

Throughout the years, various individuals have claimed to have injured or killed the Jersey Devil. In 1887, an unidentified elderly man at the Mount Holly Fair in Burlington County told the *Newark Sunday Call* a family legend. He said the story was explained to him as a boy by his father, who was a young man at the time of the occurrence, sometime in the early nineteenth century. The newspaper informant said his grandfather went out to investigate an unsual noise in the barnyard, and within a few minutes, he crashed through the kitchen door and "rolled in on the floor all in a heap. He was as pale as the inside of a flour bag and his teeth chattered and eyes staring." He could barely whisper to his wife that the Jersey Devil was in the barnyard. Seemingly undaunted, she grabbed her flax beetle and stormed out the door. But her confidence was short-lived. In no time she rushed back in the door, screaming and looking as pale as her husband. The two soon regained their composure, however, and armed with a gun and flax beetle, they returned to the barnyard—but the Jersey Devil had fled.

Rumors soon began circulating around the area of how the Jersey Devil was sucking blood from one of the horses in the barnyard, and how the woman broke the beast's wing with her flax beetle. She even proudly showed off her flax beetle, complete with blood stains.

During the famed Jersey Devil appearances of 1909, the death of the creature and an injury to it were reported in two different incidents. William Wasso, a trackwalker on the electric railroad between Clayton and Newfield, told Clayton Councilman R.L. Campbell that the Jersey Devil had been blasted to death by high voltage when its long, slimy tail came into contact with the third rail. And in the Pines outside of Pleasantville, Howard Campbell, a lineman for the Delaware and Atlantic Telephone Company, was chased up a telegraph pole by the Jersey

Devil. Theodore Hackett, a fellow lineman, was drawn to the scene by Campbell's screams, and he shot the Devil in the wing. Screaming in pain, the beast, who had the head of a horse, wings of a bat, and a long, rat-like tail, disappeared into the woods. Since 1909, there have been a number of reports claiming the Jersey Devil was dead, but the creature continues to appear. About the time of World War I, what was supposed to be the Jersey Devil's body was placed on display in Paterson. However, few details are known about this incident.

In 1925, a garish account of the Jersey Devil's demise was reported by William Hyman of Greenwich Township, Gloucester County.

Hyman claimed that after finding the creature eating chickens, he chased it and, during a wrestling match with the creature, shot it dead. Hyman displayed the carcass for the curious, who visited by the hundreds. In his description of the creature to the *Woodbury Daily Times*, Hyman said it was as big as an Airedale, with black fur, and it hopped like a kangaroo. Its front legs, he said, were longer than the rear, which were short and crouched, the hind feet having four webbed toes. Its yellow eyes were open in death, and Hyman said, "Its jaw is neither dog, wolf, nor coyote." He added an odd detail about its teeth: "Its crushers in the lower jaws have four prongs into which the upper teeth fit perfectly."

In late October 1925, Morrell Langley found a mysterious body in a tree on the Franklinville Road outside of Swedesboro, and a number of residents thought this strange carcass was the Jersey Devil. The body, which appeared to have been dead for about a month, was two and a half feet long and one foot high. Its back feet and legs resembled those of a cat, and its front legs looked something like those of a monkey. The creature's mouth was a bony structure. Langley turned the body over to Harry Finzer, of Franklinville, who intended to present the body to the University of Pennsylvania for an autopsy. Like so many other accounts of the Jersey Devil, this is where the story ends.

In October 1957, at Hampton Furnace in the Pine Barrens, foresters with the New Jersey Department of Conservation and Economic Development found some burned, "eerie remains" at the edge of a cranberry bog. These consisted of a partial skeleton, claws, feathers, bone particles, and some unidentified hind legs. Opinion was divided as to whether these fragmentary remains were left as a prank, an old trophy, or were the dismembered body of the Jersey Devil.

Ron F. Stephensen, of Forked River, proprietor of Skipper's Roadside in Waretown, has hanging on display in his restaurant a strange bone which some people think is the remains of the Jersey Devil, though the creature has been seen numerous times since the discovery of this bone. Stephensen and his family were on a camping trip in the Pine Barrens around 1966, when his son saw something odd protruding from the earth. The family carefully excavated what looks like a misshapen skull. Stephensen reports that customers are very curious about the strange object on display.

A Price on His Head

From time to time, individuals or organizations have offered rewards for the capture of the Jersey Devil. During the 1909 episode, Robert D. Carson, Superintendent of the Philadelphia Zoo, promised $10,000 to anyone who captured the Jersey Devil, and he further vowed to build a special exhibit for the creature. Jacob F. Hope, working in collusion with hoaxter Norman Jefferies, put up $500 during that same year. He claimed that the Jersey Devil was a rare Australian vampire. George Hartzell, who was also interested in obtaining the Jersey Devil, offered $50.

Tongue in cheek, the *Philadelphia Press* in 1909 offered $30,000 for the Jersey Devil—$25,000 for the Jersey Devil himself, and $5,000 for a signed interview with whoever brought in the creature. One humorous anecdote involving some of the 1909 reward money concerned Walter S. Flynt, of George Street in New Brunswick. His son came flying into the house, exclaiming that a strange beast, possibly the Jersey Devil, was in the yard. Flynt, envisioning quick wealth, seized a broom and ran out the door to effect the capture. Unfortunately for Flynt, this Jersey Devil turned out to be an opossum.

In 1960, with an eye toward bringing more people into the business district, the Broadway Improvement Association of Camden pledged $10,000 for the live delivery of the Jersey Devil. They added into the bargain the resolution to build a special display area.

By far, the largest reward ever offered for the Jersey Devil was from Harry Hunt, of Hunt Brothers Circus in Florence. In 1960 and again in 1976, he offered $100,000 for the capture, alive and unharmed, of the Jersey Devil.

To date, no one has had to pay up.

Police Involvement

Since 1909, when Officer Sackville of the Bristol Police discharged his service revolver at the Jersey Devil in the wee hours of Sunday, January 17th, at the start of the Devil's famous urban visitations, police agencies have, by the nature of their work, been involved in many of the Jersey Devil legends. Even today, police continue to receive calls about New Jersey's famous resident. Edward Early, who served as Chief of Police of Plumstead Township, Ocean County, from 1957 to 1968, remembers being called on during Jersey Devil incidents, and two of the most unusual ones stand out in his memory.

During the summer of 1966, as Officer Early has told the authors, he received a call from a frightened family who said the Jersey Devil was prowling in their backyard. One member of the household told Early that he saw the outhouse door opened, something lurking in the back-yard, and hoofprints on the ground. Early's conclusion was that these were horseprints and shadows, but the family insisted that they were the work of the Jersey Devil. That night, they slept with baseball bats in their hands.

About a year later, the second incident took place: Two men and a woman were walking through the woods when they saw a weird beast with the head of a pig. Certain they had encountered the Jersey Devil, they called Early, who rushed to the scene and found them "really shook up," but the creature was nowhere to be found. When word of this incident spread, quite a few teenagers in nearby Hanover Township refused to go out at night. Grateful parents implored Early to publicize any additional sightings of this type, because it kept their children in at night.

Two South Jersey journalists recall several incidents of fleeting contact between police and a creature that some called the Jersey Devil. Ann Waters, who was working at the Camden *Courier-Post* in 1965, covered a sighting at the Glassboro Fish and Wildlife Management Area, in Clayton. Police were called to the scene, and Waters reported that police shot in the direction of violent crashing in the woods about 3:00 A.M. One day in the early 1970s, as Fritz Davis of *The Jersey Devil* newspaper remembers, there was an occurrence involving the West Windsor Township police. Officers in a patrol car were returning from a call outside their jurisdiction, traveling along Route 539, when they saw a mother and her young daughter standing by a car alongside the road. When the officers stopped, the hysterical mother said that a creature had darted out of the woods, seized a handful of the child's hair, and disappeared into the woods again. Some people disbelieved the story; however, as one of the policemen said, "People can laugh all they want to, but the hair was pulled out of the child's head."

Officer Edward O. Herbert, Jr. has certainly seen some unusual things in his many years with the Ocean County Sheriff's Department, and previously with the Ocean County Park Police. In the summer of 1979, Herbert and a number of other area residents independently saw a large, mountain lion–like cat in the vicinity of the Miller Air Park in Berkeley Township. In fact, Herbert was stopped by a visitor from Africa, who asked if Herbert realized that a lion was roaming the vicinity. The visitor told Herbert that the tracks he had seen nearby were definitely like those of a lion. Thinking that this creature was an escapee from Great Adventure Park, Herbert investigated, but was told no wild animals were missing. Some residents armed themselves and searched the woods for the mystery cat, yet the creature had disappeared.

That fall, there was an interesting postscipt to this episode. A hunter shot a deer that had long, deep claw marks down its back, as though a predator of considerable size had grabbed it. The hunter told Herbert that either the lion had returned or these claw marks were the work of the Jersey Devil.

Some police take Jersey Devil sightings seriously. Others find them amusing, and still others consider the Jersey Devil an annoyance. Trooper Al Potter of the New Jersey State Police falls into the latter group. After the strange loss of livestock along the Mullica River in 1966, Potter expressed his pique: "With all the homicides we solved, all anybody ever wants to hear about is that Jersey Devil."

VII

PRANKS, TALL TALES, AND SECOND-HAND STORIES

With such a rich and varied history, the Jersey Devil has caused generations to react to his presence and to make him the stuff of their legends and games. Many pranks involving the Jersey Devil have been pulled on the unsuspecting, and because his presence is so strong, many tall tales have exaggerated and perpetuated his exploits. Stories about him have worked their way into the folktale process as well.

Pranks and Hoaxes

In the early 1960s, it looked like the Jersey Devil had struck again at a number of spots in rural Salem County. Laundry hung out to dry was found scattered about the yards, tools were inexplicably moved, cars mysteriously appeared up on curbs, and road signs were twisted awry. Residents were alarmed and thought it was the Devil up to his old tricks once more. Eventually, however, the local police found out the incidents were not supernatural, but the work of local teenagers.

This was not the first time a prank had been pulled in the name of the Jersey Devil. Periodically, both old and young have been responsible for Jersey Devil jokes. The creature's basic characteristics lend themselves well to human playfulness, but modern pranks prove there is still deep-rooted interest in the Jersey Devil legend.

Mary Catherine Kennedy recalls the Jersey Devil prank perpetrated by her father, William Felter, during 1964. Around the tree in their front yard on Bay Avenue, in Barnegat, her father made a track of fake footprints. Though the tree was already terminally diseased, Felter said the death of the tree was caused by the Jersey Devil footprints. The neighborhood children were convinced.

Then there was the rookie policeman, new to the Pinelands area, whom other members of the force jokingly warned to be extremely careful while at work in the more remote sections—because of the Jersey Devil. The officer took them seriously and kept his car's dome light on constantly whenever he was in these areas. His car burned out far more than its share of dome lightbulbs.

The Jersey Devil is a natural subject for pranks on and by South Jersey campers. Seasoned campers frequently howl, thrash about in the woods, and otherwise attempt to scare their greener counterparts. In May 1978, Bill Thompson (whose Lenape Native American name is "Listens-to-Whippoorwill") perpetrated an elaborate hoax on a group of campers along the Wading River at Bodine Field in Wharton State Forest. Thompson and two others who also knew the Jersey Devil legend well were leading a camping trip. Around the campfire, the trio entertained the others with eerie tales of the Devil to cause a little good-natured terror that night. After everyone had bedded down, Thompson and his cohorts crept off into the woods and began howling. The three leaders had told the campers that the Jersey Devil could walk on water, so Thompson took a canoe paddle and started whacking it noisily on the surface of the river. Then, he held a flashlight pointed upward against his face and slumped over, which gave him a ghostly aura in the dark. By this time, the campers had awakened and made their way to the river bank to see what was happening. One girl fled back, jumping across the campfire in fright.

In addition, there was that night the Jersey Devil "appeared" to the campers at Smithville who were history buffs rehearsing a re-enactment of some military battles. One of these thespians had a Jersey Devil costume and terrorized a number of his comrades by charging in and out of the tents after they had retired for the night. When this same group re-enacted the 200th anniversary of the Battle of Chestnut

Neck in October 1978, they heard mysterious screams in the woods—but that time, there was no prankster.

Around 1963, Richard Andwake lived near a Cherry Hill orchard, in which there was an abandoned shack consisting of one room and an attic. The local people claimed the shack was 100 years old. Word had it that a farmer had been murdered there. They believed that the Jersey Devil lurked about the place, and this belief was strengthened when one day a group of children found the words "JERSEY DEVIL" burned one inch deep into the wooden door. The children liked to frighten newcomers to the area by showing them this terrifying logo; however, none of the kids ever ventured there after dark.

Mandy Herbert, of Green Bank, talks about her experiences with the Jersey Devil pranks in the mid-1970s, when she was a girl. As she recounted to the authors, "When I moved down here from Brick Town (in the mid-1970s), I asked the other kids who the Jersey Devil was. They said that he appeared every seven years and ate three little boys and three little girls, and that he was due to appear again shortly. Sometime after that, some kids were out in a car and said the Jersey Devil, with bright red eyes, landed on top of their car roof and thumped all over it. Kids love to tell Jersey Devil stories."

Clyde Birdsall, a retired New Jersey State Forest Ranger from Sweetwater, got a surprise going to work one morning in May 1976. There, in front of the door at the Atsion Ranger Station, stood the Jersey Devil. The thing was eight feet tall, had a five-foot-around belly, weighed several hundred pounds—and was composed of papier-mâché, wood, and chicken wire, complete with battery-powered, flashing lights for eyes.

Birdsall thought he remembered hearing about such a Jersey Devil appearing in a parade the previous Halloween, and he surmised that someone had been pulling the thing around behind their car, trying to create an incident, then left it by the front door of the Ranger Station. Birdsall and several others dragged the huge Devil into a six-foot-high enclosure, topped with three strands of barbed wire. Next day, the thing was gone, though there was no sign of forced entry or marks in the sand. To this day, no one knows whatever became of this "Jersey Devil."

Tall Tales

Tall tales are periodically told about any creature who has found its way into the folklore of an area. William McMahon, in *Pine Barrens Legends, Lore and Lies,* tells one about how the Jersey Devil had a hand in setting up a dual highway along a road in the Pine Barrens' Wharton Tract. The road, which ran from Long-a-Coming (now Berlin) to Tuckerton, was not wide enough for stagecoaches to pass all the way from Atsion to Batsto. Finally, the volume of stage traffic increased so much that another lane about a mile long was built along this stretch. There were those who claimed the Jersey Devil was responsible for this new road, however, because one twilight night, when a stagecoach encountered the Jersey Devil standing square in the roadway, both driver and horses panicked, and the swath they cut through the woods created the new lane.

In *New Jersey: A Guide to its Past and Present*, Howard Patterson reported his encounter with the Jersey Devil. According to Patterson, custodian of the school in Perrineville in the 1930s, "It was a foggy night, when I saw him all aglow, just a few feet off the road. I walked right up and put out my hand. Found an old tree with two knotty arms, lit up like a fox fire." Frank E. Hires, of *The Atlantic City Press,* adds two other tall tales of the Jersey Devil. One is about a Margate man who claimed to have wrestled with the creature. The other concerns a Pleasantville man who blasted the Jersey Devil with both barrels of his shotgun at point-blank range, only to have the Jersey Devil casually fly away.

Henry Charlton Beck, in *More Forgotten Towns of Southern New Jersey*, adds to this Jersey Devil tall tale tradition with an interesting 1930s story of a place called "The Blue Hole," not far from where the Great Egg Harbor River crosses Piney Hollow Road west of Hammonton. According to local tradition, the Blue Hole is bottomless and the Jersey Devil lurks there, waiting to pull in the unwary.

In February 1976, the Blue Hole tale was still alive and well. Two teenage boys told Frances and Joseph Shute that the Jersey Devil lived in the Blue Hole, and that he was the demon who might draw the unfortunate down into its depths. One of the boys claimed his uncle told him about some weird Jersey Devil experiences he had while camping

at a nearby Boy Scout camp. The uncle said the footbridge built in the 1930s was already in ruins when he used to camp there, but the Jersey Devil's pounding hooves could be heard crossing the nonexistent bridge every night.

A long story reported by the well-known South Jersey writer Ed Brown in Medford's *The Central Record* recounted a 1978 incident at a bar in Tabernacle. The whole thing was brought to Brown's attention by a man who burst into the newspaper office with some last-minute news just as the next week's edition was going to press. Nervously looking over his shoulder as Brown calmed him with herbal tea, the man related a frightening event he had just witnessed. The bar patrons were enjoying themselves this Saturday night when they heard an "unearthly scream" coming from the parking lot. As people dashed out the door, they were confronted by the Jersey Devil. The thing had a horse's head, a dragon's body, and violently flapped its huge wings. Strangely enough, it also wore a t-shirt, and it "squawked like a fifteen-hundred-pound chicken." After circling the parking lot for a few minutes, this apparition swooped off in the direction of the Pine Barrens. The bar offered drinks on the house to calm the rattled patrons, and Ed Brown wrote this for *The Central Record*'s April Fool issue.

The Jersey Devil is at times a creature of legend, or of pranksters' fun, and the source of stories told so often their origins blend into folklore. The long tradition of the Jersey Devil encompasses many tales, often transmitted in the characteristic word-of-mouth way.

Second-hand Stories

Second-hand stories are stories for which no eyewitnesses can be found. Sometimes, these tales include incidents of the Devil attacking or abducting humans.

Elizabeth Lang, of Moorestown, related a story passed down through her family for generations: Once upon a time, a farmer from the Millville area had a large field, surrounded by woods, perfect for growing corn. In fact, by the time he had finished sowing the last row of corn, the first rows would already have sprouted. Each ear of this legendary corn grew to be some 20 inches long. He was successful with the field for many years. Then, one year, he noticed that each morning, a row of corn had been consumed. The puzzled farmer also found strange footprints in his field. Annoyed at this nightly pillage, he, his 14-year-old son, and a neighbor decided to spend the night in the cornfield to catch the marauder red-handed. After dusk, the three, each carrying a lantern, walked single file toward the field.

As they reached the corn, the night grew darker, and the trio became separated as a dense fog rolled in. Searching for his companions, the farmer heard bloodcurdling screams coming from somewhere behind him. Frightened for his son and his friend, the man began running toward the screams. Finally he made out two lanterns bobbing in the wind. He rushed toward them and saw that the lanterns were hanging, unattended, from the low branches of a tree. Then, out of the dark fog, something tall and dark, with huge wings, swooped down on him, knocking him to the ground. He could not see what it was, but as the wings brushed his face, he thought he smelled sulfur. In panic, the man scrambled to his feet and fled home.

When the poor man ran through his kitchen doorway, his wife nearly fainted: he was as pale as a ghost. Terrified, the farmer spent the rest of the night quaking in his house. The next morning, the entire neighborhood joined in a search for the couple's missing son and the other man, but all they ever found were the two lanterns, still hanging, abandoned, on the branches. The neighborhood had no doubt the Jersey Devil had struck again.

Daniel Rich, a New York City bookstore manager, told the authors of a story that circulated around 1960, when he was a child in Pitman:

Two deer hunters were camping in the Pines. The night was clear and they had a good fire going. They were talking about the Jersey Devil and belittling the stories they had heard. They talked for awhile until around midnight, when one of the hunters started to put the fire out, but was prevented from doing so by a strong breeze that totally snuffed the flames out for him. Both hunters were startled by horrible screams coming from their left about 300 feet away. When they looked they saw a bluish mist drifting towards them, in the center of which were two piercing red eyes that never blinked as the mist drifted closer. When the mist was almost on them they saw the outline of huge wings and immediately thought of the creature they had been mocking. One of the hunters broke for the car parked on a small dirt road a few hundred yards away. The other man dashed into the woods. The hunter heading for the car heard something lumbering and crashing behind him. He made it to the car and drove off as quickly as possible, as something bumped against the back of the car. He drove to the nearest bar and phoned the police. When they arrived he told them that some large, winged creature had attacked his campsite. The police didn't give him much credence, but drove out with him to the site. There they found the campfire blazing again and no sign of disorder. The party went off looking for the missing hunter, but didn't find him. They took the hunter down to the police station and only in the strong light did they see the claw marks that ran straight down the hunter's back trunk. The next day they searched again for the missing hunter, but they never found him.

Thomas Tiernan, of Metuchen, heard about a Jersey Devil sighting in the Pine Barrens north of Atlantic City in the summer of 1975. Six men were camping, and four of them went for a walk around sunset. They found a clearing dotted with a number of mounds of earth 12 to 15 feet high. The men climbed on top of one and began talking. As it got darker and darker, several high-pitched, strange cries rang out, and between two of the mounds, a man-like creature appeared. One of the men announced they were in an area of frequent Jersey Devil sightings. The four ran back to the campsite, where they told the other two what they had seen and heard. All six spent the night in their tents, wide awake and with large campfires burning.

VIII

THE JERSEY DEVIL IN OTHER STATES

While the Jersey Devil usually is seen in his home state, he has visited New York, Maryland, California, Canada, Pennsylvania, Delaware, and Texas. It seems the creature is able to wander across state lines with great facility.

Pennsylvania: Bucks County

Interestingly enough, one of the first appearances the Jersey Devil made during that famous week in January 1909 was in Bucks County, Pennsylvania, in the town of Bristol. Very early in the morning of Sunday, January 17th, there were three separate incidents involving several different people.

First, John McOwen, of Bath Street, was awakened by his baby daughter's crying. When he entered her room, he heard strange noises coming from outside the house. They sounded "like the scratching of a phonograph needle before the music begins." Looking out the window, McOwen saw a strange creature, which looked something like an eagle, hopping along the towpath of the Delaware Division Canal.

Officer James Sackville, who later became Bristol's chief of police, also had a startling experience this same night, around 2:00 A.M. Sackville was out on patrol when his attention was drawn by barking dogs. The officer was looking around when the Jersey Devil suddenly

appeared in front of him. The large creature had wings and strange features, and it emitted terrible screams. Sackville pulled his gun and raced toward the monster, shooting at it, but the thing flew off into the night.

E.W. Minster, Bristol's postmaster, also saw the Devil at about the same hour. Hearing a "supernatural sound," he looked out to see a strange creature flying over the river. He said it resembled a large crane, and it glowed like a firefly. Its head had ram horns, and its neck was long and thin. The creature let out a strange cry, which sounded like a cross between a squawk and a whistle.

The next morning, footprints two inches long and one foot apart were found all over the town. Thomas Holland, of Buckley Street, and James Lawler, of Bath Street, both found numerous clear footprints in the snow in their yards. An Officer Munchnoff, however, apparently was disgusted by the situation, claiming that had he been on duty instead of Officer Sackville, he would have shot the Jersey Devil.

On the night of Thursday, January 21st, the Jersey Devil appeared in Wycombe, also in Bucks County, where a group of men were standing around discussing the rash of strange incidents occurring that week in the Delaware Valley. Most of the group had read the Doylestown *Daily Republican,* which asserted the whole affair was caused by an excellent supply of Jersey applejack that year. Suddenly, unusual noises came from Thompson's Lumber Yard nearby. The men were "paralyzed with fear" when out of the woods flew what they later described as a "monster, part animal, part bird, part buzzard." The creature flew around the sky in circles, then soared off into the night. The men were so stunned they could not agree on its size—some said it was 9 feet long, while others said it was as large as 20 feet. The creature possessed fiery eyeballs, long wings, feathers, and menacing teeth several inches long. There was one thing on which all the men in the group did agree—the *Daily Republican* was wrong in its assessment of the Jersey Devil.

Chester, Delaware County

In 1909, sometime during the night of January 19th, and into the early morning hours of the 20th, the Jersey Devil made his appearance in

Chester, Delaware County. Nat Thompson, of the Chester Enameling Company, 15th and Earey Streets, showed reporters from the *Chester Times* many tracks near the composition houses of his plant. He pointed out that the tracks stopped and started again some 500 yards away, just over the fence of the Chester Rural Cemetery. "Whatever kind of animal, beast or bird it is, I am sure that the theory that it has wings is correct," Thompson concluded. He promised that his watchman would be keeping a sharp lookout for future appearances. The *Chester Times* reported that many local residents "are much excited and are guarding their children and chicken coops with great care."

Thompson speculated that the strong odor of banana oil, which was used in quantity during the Enamel Company's process, might have attracted the Jersey Devil. But there was no banana oil in the picture on the night of the 21st, around 10:30 P.M., when a respected Chester citizen heard strange noises on the shed roofs of Robinson's Brickyard. The clatter quickly changed to a scuffling sound in the middle of Eagle Street, and suddenly, out of the fog, "there arose a strange-looking animal—half-beast and half-bird—with wings like a bat and a long tail the end of which looked like the point of an arrow." By the glare of the electric lights, the man observed the creature flying low through the fog along Eagle Street. As it neared the elevated railroad, "it seemed to rise like a big airship" and soared across the tracks just as the northbound express was passing, causing the engineer to blast repeatedly on his whistle. The Jersey Devil was then seen fluttering over City Hall, and it landed near the school at 3rd and Jeffrey Streets. Several policemen then chased it up Commerce Street, where it disappeared into the fog in the backyard of Thomas Marshall's funeral parlor. While officers were pursuing the creature, they found numerous footprints, and neighbors reported hearing the flapping of large wings and the racket of strange feet. After this appearance, Chris Kautz, gatekeeper at the Market Street station in West Chester, Chester County, announced he would carry a sharp razor to defend the station against any strange invader.

About 2:00 A.M. in the morning of January 22nd, J. Vernon Williams, Roadmaster for Middletown Township, Delaware County, was awakened by dogs barking outside the window. Looking out, he saw the dogs circling a strange animal which they seemed afraid to attack. When Williams opened the window, however, the creature fled.

Daybreak of the 22nd revealed many torn telephone wires in the Tenth Ward of Chester, and the telltale footprints in the snow. Around this time, the Jersey Devil also shocked Daniel Flynn of Leiperville, north of Chester, on Chester Pike. Flynn said, "It was coming out of a yard when I first saw it and when the thing espyed me it ran up the pike on its hind legs faster than the speed of an automobile. The thing, which had skin like an alligator, stood on its hind feet and was about six feet tall."

Philadelphia

The city of Philadelphia did not escape the visit of the Jersey Devil in 1909, either. For several days during this astounding week, numerous residents of Pennsylvania's largest city observed the Jersey Devil. Several people, including Martin Burns, saw the Jersey Devil at Beach Street and Fairmount Avenue, and William Becker, of the Germantown section, announced he threw stones at the Devil on Lime Kiln Pike. In response to the numerous tracks, W.H. Cantrell said, "Now I hate to talk about this—all the fellows at the office will be laughing at me—but the tracks are there sure enough. I'll wager too that the thing that made the tracks walked on two legs."

Mrs. J.H. White, of the 1500 block of Ellsworth Street, experienced one of the more traumatic sightings in 1909. At 4:00 P.M. one afternoon, she went into the backyard to take clothes off the line, and observed a strange thing in the corner of the yard. As she walked closer to get a better look, it rose to a full six feet in height. The creature's body was covered with an alligator-like skin, and it began to spew flames from its mouth. Mrs. White screamed uncontrollably, then passed out. Her husband, a local insurance agent, dashed out the door, seized a clothes prop, and charged the Jersey Devil as it clambered over a fence and ran up an alley leading to 16th Street, all the while shooting flames from its mouth.

Mr. White stopped his pursuit to call the family physician, who worked over the unconscious Mrs. White for a full hour before she could be revived. At about the same time, a 16th Street trolley motor-man, unaware of the Whites' experience, saw a strange, fire-breathing creature dash across the tracks near Washington Avenue.

Lyndell, Chester County

"JERSEY DEVIL ROAMING AT LARGE IN LYNDELL AREA EXCITES NEIGHBORHOOD" blazed the headline of the *Coatesville Record* on January 21, 1932. Both the *Record* and the *Daily Local News* of West Chester carried details of the strange sighting, while this whole section of Chester County remained on alert.

John McCandless, a Swarthmore nurseryman, was directing his crew of several workers from the Upper Bank Nurseries of Media in digging up trees in the Lyndell-Dorlan vicinity when they heard a groaning sound coming from the other side of a small ridge. McCandless and one of the men looked around and found the noise was coming from behind a small bush. The men were terrified when the Jersey Devil "jumped over a high clump of bushes and came at them." The two fled to a nearby farmhouse, where they borrowed a shotgun. The farmer told them he had seen the thing prowling about his property in the moonlight several weeks before, but he had been too terrified to shoot at it. McCandless and the worker returned to the site, where they found mysterious tracks in the mud, but, again, the creature was gone.

McCandless later told the *Daily Local News*, "It was about the height of a man and was without clothing of any kind. Its skin was a yellow-ish-gray in color and its face was more horrible than that of any animal I have ever seen pictured. Its head, hands and feet appeared to be un-usually large and it stood partially erect when walking. I could not say whether it was man or beast." The workman with McCandless ex-claimed, "Man, that wasn't nothin' human! It growled and groaned like a wildcat and made chills run up and down your back just to hear it. It didn't walk either; it crawled and it crawled mighty fast."

The next day, McCandless, Josiah Hoopes, and the workmen returned to the site, armed for a search. They covered the entire area but were unable to find anything.

Almost immediately, the incident created national interest, and front page articles appeared across the nation. Four newspapermen banded together to conduct their own investigation. They tended to be skeptical of the whole business, but they still carried an antique sword with them—just in case! They introduced their episode with the following words, "Oh, where, oh, where, is the phantom at? Oh, where, oh, where, can he be?" With this as their signature, the four headed off into the wilds "to personally interview his Satanic majesty the Jersey Devil or the member of his royal household said to inhabit that peculiar section of Chester County." After hours of slogging through mud, and tearing their clothing on brambles and bushes, the reporters returned without having been successful in their mission.

In November 1945, *The Record* of Coatesville, Pennsylvania, announced, "JERSEY DEVIL RETURNS FOR A LITTLE VISIT." As both this paper and the *Daily Local News* of West Chester were quick to report, a reappearance of the Jersey Devil in the Sheep Hill area of North Coventry Township touched off a wave of strong local reaction, including posses, gun discharges, and even an automobile accident.

Some people thought the creature was a panther, but Peter J. Filkosky, of Kennett Square, State Game Protector for Chester County, said no panthers had been in that area for over 50 years. In general, people throughout the region became alarmed following the mysterious disappearance of chickens and turkeys, as well as the discovery of a dead gray fox.

Among those who saw the infamous monster was Thomas Rhodes, whose eyewitness description matches those of other witnesses. He said the creature was larger than a fox, with a sleek black coat, long body, short and pointed ears, and a long, thin tail. Claude Reinhart, of Pottstown, said the Jersey Devil sounded like "a man screaming as loud as he could." Lester Thompson, of Douglassville, described the sequence of the calls: "It starts sort of low-pitched, gives a couple of short bursts first then it lets her rip." Most people who have heard Devil sounds characterized them as somewhere between the screams of a man and the cries of a baby.

Several of the witnesses also attested to the Jersey Devil's jumping ability. John Wojack, of Pottstown, said, "It bounded away in leaps of at least ten feet in length each." John Hipple, a Montgomery County farmer, took some shots at the elusive creature and saw it "leap about twenty feet in the air, and, screaming, disappeared. . . It was like a big cat."

With this rash of sightings, people started picking up their children at school bus stops and keeping them in at night. But other citizens took more aggressive action, which soon led to things getting out of hand. One group of men searched the woods and fields one night during this period until 3:30 A.M. They were the first of a series of increasingly active posses. Officer John J. Boyle, of the North Coventry Township Police, called for a posse to gather at his house one morning, and Peter Filkosky was among them. Boyle requested the men bring "rifles and shotguns and 'coon dogs, if possible." What this posse and a number of informal hunting parties succeeded in doing over the next few days was filling the woods with a great number of discharged rounds. The searchers' zeal caused them to fire at just about anything that moved, creating quite a hazard. Filkosky observed, "I think there is more danger from stray shots and shotgun pellets than from the animal itself."

Mrs. Edward Creger, who lived in the midst of this zone of gunfire at Sheep Hill, echoed Filkosky's sentiments. Kept awake until all hours by the sounds of gunfire and flocks of searchers tramping across her land, she became annoyed. "Maybe I'll start some shooting myself, if this nonsense doesn't stop," she warned.

As Filkosky had cautioned, the injury reports started to roll in. William J. Brandel, 18, of Pottstown, was wounded in the thigh by a bullet, and Bettey Hart, 17, of Douglassville, was hit in the left arm. Two other young people got themselves injured in a somewhat more spectacular manner. A group of youths were motoring down a small road in the area, searching the woods for the Jersey Devil, when to their surprise and pain, they found out too late they were on a dead-end road. Their vehicle smashed through a barrier at the end of the lane, hopped a five-foot embankment, and plunged to an injurious halt. Ivan Leaman, Jr., 18, and Irene Petzer, 21, both of Pottstown, were treated at the Pottstown Hospital for cuts, brush burns, and one cut lip.

The Sheep Hill incident had come full circle. Police called for an end to posses and, in fact, began searching cars traveling into the area for firearms. They said anyone found carrying a loaded weapon in his vehicle would be prosecuted, and as a last attempt to capture the Jersey Devil, the police resorted to the safer method of leaving bear traps.

"The Pottstown Monster"

In March 1973, eastern Montgomery County, Pennsylvania, was visited by a mysterious creature some called the "Pottstown Monster," but which bore a striking resemblance to the Jersey Devil. This strange creature broke into several chicken coops and rabbit hutches over a period of several weeks, ripping up the poor animals but apparently never eating any. It had bright red eyes, and some people reported that the thing was cat-like. Others said it was much larger, walked on its hind legs, and was a reddish or black color. Numerous residents of the Pottstown area combed the woods with guns, and though some of the police said the creature was a dog or some other well-known animal, one woman commented, "I don't care what anyone says, I'm keeping my doors locked until they find it." A few even sought to create some sort of tourist attraction out of the episode.

Delaware: Wilmington

Delaware was also visited by the Jersey Devil during the famous week in January 1909, when he soared southward into that state. On January 27, 1909, Wilmington's paper, *The Morning News,* announced, "THE MONSTER HAS ARRIVED," as the state began to feel the effects of the mysterious visitor.

During this amazing week, numerous footprints turned up in the Wilmington snows, just as they did throughout the rest of the Delaware Valley. Many witnesses saw these tracks, and citizens of northern Delaware were puzzled and at least a little afraid.

The first person in this area to observe the prints was Lewis G. Spence, who found them in the railroad freight yards at Todd's Cut. They resembled those of a small colt, ran through the yards for the length of a city block, and had no clear beginning or end.

Mrs. Emma Pier, of North Harrison Street, discovered unusual patterns of prints in her yard, and they also popped up elsewhere in Wilmington. Some of the prints looked as if the strange visitor had only one front foot and one hind foot. Others appeared to belong to a four-footed animal, but in some places, only the front prints were seen! (Was it walking on its front feet?) As a result of these occurrences, to cite *The Morning News*, "men were resting at arms."

One morning at 4:00 A.M., William Thompson, a milkman, was driving his wagon into Wilmington for his morning deliveries. Near the gate of Shellpot Park, he saw something in the dark. At first, he thought it was a calf, but then it reared up on its hind feet. It had a "long neck, long tail, long nose, short forelegs with claws at the end, and long back legs upon which it was sitting." It was shaped like a kangaroo, and its red eyes gleamed through the dark. Thompson tried to move closer for a better look—then, the Devil barked at him like a dog and charged his milk wagon. The man whipped the horse, and the clattering wagon took off at full speed south toward the city; when Thompson peered over his shoulder, the beast was bounding up Penny Hill. But Thompson, in his flight, did not stop until he reached 10th and Market Streets in downtown Wilmington, some miles away. Understandably, he told *The Morning News* he had never before had an experience like that—and he did not care to have one like it again!

That night, around 11:00 P.M., Paul Taylor, John C. Hayes, and John C. Braff were returning from a lodge meeting when they saw something in the darkness along Concord Avenue. Knowing that some eerie creature was prowling the city streets, they "beat it while their shoes were good."

The Jersey Devil then created excitement in the area of Front and Union Streets. Three members of the Union Fire Company, Leonard Lynch, Charles McGaughey, and John Chambers, startled by unusual noises coming from an old barn next to the firehouse, rushed over to investigate. They thereby met the Jersey Devil, who sprang out, and, with a single leap, cleared the ticket office of the nearby baseball park and disappeared into the surrounding dark. The astonished firefighters swore the Devil had jumped at least 25 feet. Lynch, Officer John McAteer, and several others searched the area, but they found only a half-eaten pumpkin and footprints. They described the prints as similar to an unshod pony's, but with what appeared to be toes.

Members of a tent revival meeting housed in the cold snow of Union Park were disturbed by these events. After hearing the strange noises and observing the footprints, one woman took her children and fled to the shelter of the more solid Park Hotel.

Wilmington's newspapers treated these sightings with differing editorial voices. *The Morning News* tended to carry the various Jersey Devil incidents and was careful to play up the sensational, but *Every Evening* took a more conservative view. A kind of newspaper war ensued. *Every Evening* bewailed:

> Reports exploited sensationally by foolish newspapers are having harmful influence on the young minds of children. Many of them believe the silly stories they hear, with the result that a large number of children are wrought up to a state of excitement which affects their sleep and may impair their health.

The causes of this phenomenon, the paper claimed, were the superstitious, who overreacted to seeing strange tracks (they seemed to agree there *were* strange things going on) and who blew things out of proportion because of the need to fill up newspaper space.

Sussex County

Thereafter, Delaware was relatively free of mysterious creatures for years, except for a strange beast known as the "Monster of Burnt Swamp," who was periodically observed strolling the remote, rural roads of Sussex County. But in August and September of 1979, Sussex County was the stage for a rash of strange occurrences.

Unusual footprints turned up throughout the eastern part of the county. Plaster casts of the 4-inch-long by 3-inch-wide footprints were made under a rabbit hutch in Millville, but the molds were inconclusive, as rain had changed the original shape of the prints. Residents of Sussex County grew alarmed as they wondered about the identity of the strange creature that had invaded their territory. Some said it was a mountain lion. Others thought it might be a bobcat, a large house cat, or even a wolf.

Interestingly, the one person who saw this creature reported it had characteristics similar to those of the Jersey Devil. One night, a Mr. Powell, of Ocean View, heard strange noises in the woods. When he investigated, he saw an unusual beast emerge from the forest and sit for about ten minutes under a security light about 100 feet away from where he was standing. The thing then hopped away in kangaroo fashion. The next morning, long scratch marks were found on the ground which, according to Powell, "somewhat resembled those of a cat."

Whatever this creature was, with his Jersey Devil–like characteristics, he prowled in the vicinity of rabbit hutches, and there was a noticeable decline in the number of wild rabbits.

Texas: Big Bird or Jersey Devil?

From October 1975 continuing into 1976, southern Texas had a series of sightings of what local residents called "Big Bird," or *Tacuache,* which is Spanish for "opossum." San Benito, Texas, one of a number of towns visited by this soaring creature, had two policemen, patrolling the streets separately, who observed the thing. Speaking for both officers, one, Arturo Padilla, said, "It more or less looked like a stork or pelican type of bird. The wingspan I guess was about like a pretty good-sized car, about fifteen feet or so. The color was white. I've done a lot of hunting but I've never seen anything like it. The thing was really oversized." Two area children told Police Chief Ted Cortez they had seen it, and they claimed it was bald-headed. Armed with a knife, Alverico Guajardo, of Brownsville, set out to find the monster, and what he encountered was a strange animal about four feet tall, with eyes that resembled silver dollars, bird-like wings, and the face of a bat.

In Rio Grande City, Sheriff Ray Alvarez said that several citizens told him they had seen a strange being sitting on top of the Starr County Courthouse. They described the beast as "half human and half bird."

Outside of San Antonio, in separate incidents, two teachers were amazed to see *Tacuache.* According to the *News—San Antonio,* one teacher saw a bird the size of a Piper Cub airplane. It looked to her like a pteranodon, a flying reptile from 160 million years ago. The other claimed the bird that buzzed her car had a huge breast and a bony structure. The school administration admonished the teachers not to talk about these sightings to the children.

A number of three-toed tracks also appeared in a field outside of Harlingen. A foot long and seven inches wide, they covered a distance of 80 yards before disappearing. Two children told a reporter the tracks were made not by Big Bird, but by a hairy, ape-like beast.

According to the San Antonio *Light*, Francisco Magallanez was attacked by Big Bird in Eagle Pass. Police Captain Donald Smith told a reporter about Magallanez's terrible experience: "A creature standing about six feet tall attacked a twenty-one-year-old man at 12:45 A.M. The creature, either a bird or an animal, is described as having a brown or almost black body, bright eyes and the wings of a bat. The man says it stood on short, stubby legs and had two arms, each about 2 1/2 feet long. It had pointed ears, the face of a pig, but didn't have a snout. He says it hissed at him, took a short hop, and jumped on his shoulders. He says when it touched him, he became very hot." A doctor examined Magallanez and determined that his wounds had been caused by some unknown animal or bird.

In several counties of southern Texas, cattle were mutilated. These killings were blamed on Big Bird because of the mysterious footprints found around the bodies. Police in the area were at odds over how best

to deal with the problem: Brownsville City Police were instructed to hold their fire, while Cameron County Sheriff's Deputies were ordered to shoot on sight.

Many people in southern Texas were concerned about these sightings, but their responses varied greatly. Some residents remained indoors, and others armed themselves and threatened to shoot Big Bird on sight. A few kept maps of the sightings as a preliminary step toward a systematic Big Bird hunt. One man summoned Brownsville police after finding an unusual-looking dead bird in his yard, but it turned out to be a common variety of sea bird. In San Antonio, a television cameraman captured what he thought was Big Bird on film, but this one was only a large blue heron.

Offers of rewards for the live capture of the creature soon followed. KIRO radio, of McAllen, offered $1000, and an unnamed Houston woman also put up $500. One of the more flamboyant awards was declared by Jack Grimm, an Abilene oil man and film producer, who said he would pay $5000 for the real thing but admonished, "I don't want any brown pelicans, condors, or whooping cranes. The bird must have a wingspread in excess of 15 feet and be a species not heretofore identified—or a species thought to be extinct."

Some people tied Big Bird to the folklore of the Americas. This is not surprising. The tradition of "Thunderbird" has been a part of southwest Native American folklore for a long time. This huge bird periodically soared through the skies, bringing thunder.

Jerseyites Claim Their Own

While Big Bird crossed the Texas sky, there were those who suspected something funny was in the air. The activities of this creature reminded some people of the Jersey Devil. Certain Jerseyites claimed that Big Bird was, in fact, the monster from their own state. A tongue-in-cheek rivalry began between the Garden State and the Lone Star State over the rightful residence of the Jersey Devil.

Representatives from the private and public sectors of both states became embroiled in this good-natured squabble over the Jersey Devil's proper home. Len Sheinkin, an Atlantic City public relations expert, volunteered to lead New Jersey's claim of ownership, and formed the Concerned Citizens for the Return of the Jersey Devil. He sent a barrage of letters to prominent people asking for their help. The PR man told Sonny Schwartz of the *Atlantic City Press* that

> It's no mere coincidence that as soon as reports came out of Texas about the sudden appearance of an unnamed monster, our own Jersey Devil just as suddenly disappeared without so much as a note to the milkman to cancel deliveries. There's no doubt in my mind that we're victims of Texas devil rustlers. They'll probably rename him the Texas Devil, smack a ten-gallon hat on his noggin and turn him into some kind of crazy cowboy.
>
> Shall there be no more banshee wail in the Pine Barrens. . . no more weird sightings by the light of the full moon. . . just some run-of-the-sky flying saucers? Why this is worse than a kidnapping. It's a pure and simple case of devil napping—something you don't often catch. It's like stealing Santa Claus. Nah, worse than that. It's like somebody went to the Lone Star State and snatched its only star!

Sheinkin sent a Western Union Mailgram to Texas governor Dolph Briscoe, demanding that the Jersey Devil be returned to its rightful state. Sheinkin also mailed copies to New Jersey Governor Brendan Byrne, Pennsylvania Governor Milton Shapp, and Delaware Governor Sherman Tribbitt, hoping to win the support of the latter two states, and appealing to the regional patriotism of New Jersey's governor. None of the governors, however, chose to reply.

Even so, not all public officials turned a deaf ear to New Jersey's plight. United States Congressman William J. Hughes, of New Jersey's Second District, addressed the Texas incident in a rousing letter to Sheinkin on February 17, 1976:

> Dear Mr. Sheinkin:
>
> Thank you very much for informing me of the latest status reports of the Jersey Devil's whereabouts.
>
> Frankly, I was shocked to hear that the Devil's disappearance from South Jersey concided with its sudden reappearance in Texas. I consider this to be a matter of considerable concern and am contemplating contacting the appropriate federal authorities.
>
> I do suspect, however, that despite paltry awards and possible kidnappers, the Jersey Devil will escape and return home. In the 200 years that we

have come to know and love this creature he has invariably found his way back home to his native South Jersey haunts.

With no response coming from Texas regarding his demands, Sheinkin decided that firmer action was needed. "If this means war— so be it! Let not future generations be able to say of us that we stood idly by while one of our most cherished natural resources was wrested from his piney home and stranded on the lone prairie—quite possibly surrounded by amorous coyotes who mistook the bloodcurdling howls that are his pride and joy for their own mealy-mouthed mating call." Saying of the Texan "devil rustlers" that "I think the Governor is in ca- hoots with these galoots," Sheinkin told the *Asbury Park Press*, "We will go to Texas and surround the governor's mansion at 3:00 A.M. [date unspecified]. We will make as much noise as possible with cowbells, sirens and little old ladies from talk shows. We're pretty sure he'll give us the Devil then."

Sheinkin then proclaimed himself Commander-in-Chief of the New Jersey Expeditionary Force to Liberate the Jersey Devil from Texas, Generalissimo of the South Jersey Fleet, and Admiral of the Armies. In these roles, Sheinkin told the *Atlantic City Press*, "We are at war! We shall invade and conquer Texas. We are not only going to take back our Jersey Devil, we are going to take the whole state and rename it West Jersey."

In the spirit of this friendly feud, Mrs. Helen Leeds Walsh, of Ab- secon Highlands, told Sonny Schwartz of the *Atlantic City Press* that the Leeds family should join forces to bring the Jersey Devil back. Sheinkin announced the "invasion force" would leave Smithville, New Jersey, in April 1976, but in the meantime, to resolve the conflict peacefully, he would continue his "war of letters" and plan marches along the Atlantic City boardwalk.

Texas authorities did not choose to answer Sheinkin's correspon- dence, but they did not remain idle while Sheinkin planned his "inva- sion." An article in the Houston *American-Statesman* of March 17, 1976, entitled "Big Bird: Yankee Intruders Better Not Try to Nab Our 'Ogre,'" reported that Texans had resolved to defend the monster. Texas re- fused to acknowledge this creature could be the Jersey Devil and proudly proclaimed it "Our Bird."

According to the *American-Statesman*, Texas was not without its defenders in the United States Congress: Congressman Jake Pickle said he "would urge Governor Briscoe to use stern tactics" in the eventuality of an invasion by New Jersey. He vowed the Texas National Guard should be called out if necessary and stationed along the Red River or the Sabine. Pickle noted, "We'll loosen a flock of Texas chaparrals [roadrunner birds] on them, and they've got a beak long enough to drill an oil well, which is what they ought to be doing in New Jersey. One whack from a chaparral beak, and they'll think a real Texas Devil has got them."

The newspaper announced, "The CIA (Chaparral Intelligence Agency) has sent clandestine roadrunners to South Jersey to conduct covert spying flying operations against the Concerned Citizens for the Return of the Jersey Devil, which supports Sheinkin's invasion force." On an ecological note, it added that Ed Dutch, of the Texas Parks and Wildlife Department, warned that "Big Bird hunters could face fines up to five thousand dollars, a year in prison and confiscation of their vehicles for bothering protected birds."

Despite a report in the *American-Statesman* that the Texas National Guard was stationed along the Red and Sabine Rivers, Sheinkin planned to fly—by balloon—into Texas. On schedule, in April 1976, Sheinkin, attired in a long cape and a Lord Nelson admiral's hat, and escorted by a band and a crowd of spectators, marched across an open field at Smithville toward the huge red, white, and blue balloon. He gave a rousing speech and shouted, "On to victory!" Peggy Benham, licensed balloonist, was unable to get the balloon airborne, however, because of powerful winds blowing across the fields. One wonders what the New Jersey Expeditionary Force to Liberate the Jersey Devil would have done if the balloon had gone up.

As it turned out, the "invasion of Texas" was unnecessary. By July, the Jersey Devil had returned and was lurking in the woods of Jackson Mills. By that fall he was believed to have attacked some pigs in Salem County, and additional sightings confirmed that the Jersey Devil was, indeed, at home, where Jerseyites say he belongs.

Whether he briefly visited Texas or not is still a hotly debated issue.

IX

FOLKLORE, OPINIONS, AND THEORIES

A rich folk tradition has grown around the Jersey Devil in the 250 years of his existence. Oral tales still circulate, and many written texts have appeared in New Jersey newspapers (and with increasing frequency in national publications). Regarding the increasing scope of the Jersey Devil legend through the centuries, Pat Bontempo wrote in *New Jersey Folklife*, "The Jersey Devil has grown from a minor legend, to the best known piece of Garden State folklore, to almost a symbol of the state itself." The Devil has all the requisite earmarks of a traditional folk belief: tales are told across a large region, primarily South Jersey; several groups have kept the legend alive; the Devil tales exist with a significant amount of variants, showing that the Jersey Devil is alive both in the popular imagination and tradition; and the legend has shown some of the migration, change, and active oral retelling that are characteristic of an elaborate folk belief.

Long considered to be indigenous to the Pine Barrens, the legend also is strong along the coastal regions and, in recent years, has spread to the more urbanized parts of southern and northern New Jersey. The rich variety of Jersey Devil tales shows just how strong the tradition is. The countless birth tales, and many different sightings, experiences, and lore reveal a well-entrenched legend. The folk process definitely is visible in all this, as in any oral telling where natural change occurs in the course of a centuries-old tradition. Legends grow and change as stories are exaggerated or otherwise modified in the telling. Each generation transmits its own versions of the Jersey Devil tales to the next.

With recent sightings, current investigations and incidents, and increasing interest in folk culture, this tradition is definitely going strong.

Folklore

Varied bits of lore tell when the Jersey Devil is supposed to appear. The most common beliefs are that he turns up every seven years, or before wars, or during a full moon. Shortly before the American Revolution, for example, the Jersey Devil was seen in Salem, Cumberland, and Gloucester Counties, and he was seen before the Mexican War in Cape May County. In very late 1860 and very early 1861, the Jersey Devil flew up and down the coast, warning of the impending Civil War. In 1898, the Devil was observed in Monmouth and Atlantic Counties, just before the Spanish-American War. Even throughout the twentieth century, just before conflicts erupted, the Jersey Devil has often been seen—including December 7, 1941, Pearl Harbor Day, in Mount Holly.

In a parallel phenomenon, some hold that the Jersey Devil is active before disasters, especially serious coastal storms or major forest fires in the Pines. Supposedly, the creature appeared many times in Ocean County during May 1937, before the crash of the *Hindenberg* in Lakehurst. Some people speculate that these appearances before wars or disasters are the Jersey Devil's way of warning that the events are impending, but others take a negative view of the Devil and are convinced that he shows up to enjoy himself by watching people suffer.

According to some Jersey Devil lore, the creature does not like drawings, paintings, or other likenesses of himself. One Tuckerton woman smashed her glass Jersey Devil because she said it brought her bad luck. A well-known painting of the Jersey Devil, which hung for many years in a New Gretna tavern, mysteriously disappeared sometime in the 1960s. Around 1970, Debbie Chappine Will and her brother, Ernest, were given a bright red plastic toy figure with horns. They were told it was the Jersey Devil, and, one evening, Debbie and her brother were playing with the devil figure in a long hallway of their Hammonton home, throwing it at each other. As Ms. Will told the authors, one errant toss caused the toy to fly into a bedroom. Both children saw it slide under the bed. Debbie said that when they ran to retrieve it, "it was nowhere to be seen. There was nothing else under the bed so it couldn't have been behind something. We moved the bed and searched very thoroughly for it." Days of searching the hallway, the other rooms, and all adjacent areas yielded nothing. She adds, "To us it is still a mystery, and when we hear a tale of the Jersey Devil we still wonder to this day where it went."

Herbivore, Carnivore, or Omnivore?

Many tales even include narrative insights as to what the Jersey Devil eats. According to some accounts of his birth, the Devil's mother, father, sisters, brothers, and midwives constituted his first earthly meal. As a rule, however, his diet is considered more mundane. Many tales picture him as having an appetite for domestic animals, often chickens, and numerous accounts tell of the Devil's mutilation and slaughter of these hapless animals.

Not only does the Jersey Devil consume uncooked livestock; he seems to relish an occasional hot meal. He has been accused of blasting his fiery breath on the Mullica and Wading Rivers, so the dead fish would float to the top already steamed and ready to eat.

Perhaps the creature is an omnivore. Some South Jerseyites, however, insist that he feasts solely on the short, curly grass fern that grows in remote, damp locations. Some call this fern "The Food of the Jersey Devil." Others report the creature enjoys blueberries, a plentiful crop in the Pines.

Some residents of New Jersey's coastal region claim that deviled clams were actually named for the Jersey Devil because of his fondness for the mollusks. The fact that the creature has a sweet tooth was circulated after a number of pies left cooling on windowsills disappeared.

Theories of the Jersey Devil

Numerous theories have emerged over the years to explain the source of this puzzling phenomenon called the Jersey Devil. There is much overlapping in these opinions.

Many think the Jersey Devil is a result of mass hysteria, a condition that has plagued humanity from almost the beginning of time. There were many cases in medieval and renaissance Europe in which masses of people ran screaming through the streets, ripping off their clothes, whipping each other, and shouting the names of demons. In more recent years, there have been a number of instances in the United States, among them a "phantom anesthetist" in Mattoon, Illinois, in 1944, who sprayed gas on his victims and caused illness or paralysis. There was also an incident at a junior high school in Baltimore in 1968, when students claimed they were overcome by a mysterious gas; and in Berry, Alabama, in 1973, when both students and teachers at a local elementary school fainted, grew nauseated, collapsed, or suffered from bouts of violent scratching. Is it possible that if the Jersey Devil resulted from mass hysteria, it has a chemical origin? Ergot, a toxic plant parasite that sometimes infests edible grains, can cause hallucinations and even death. It has been speculated that the Salem witch hysteria was exacerbated by ergot in the food.

Human desire for excitement, for something out of the ordinary, might have increased interest in the Jersey Devil. Almost any youth from South Jersey who has camped in the area has been titillated by a "Jersey Devil scare," consisting of anything from a warning to watch out, to hearing strange noises in the dark night. In various locales, excitement has been stirred by people who thought the Jersey Devil was in their town.

One of the most popular theories is that the Jersey Devil was originally a retarded or deformed child. There is some feeling in the area that, years ago, whenever such a child was born there, he or she was referred to as "The Jersey Devil." A number of South Jerseyites can recall stories of these unfortunate children being kept prisoner by their families. The 1735 stories of William Leeds, Jr. point in this direction.

Numerous people believe the Jersey Devil is of animal rather than human origin. They postulate that European settlers, who were unfamiliar with the local fauna, mistook what they saw for an unearthly creature. One good possibility along these lines involves the sandhill crane, a large fowl often found in remote regions of the United States. No sandhill cranes have been seen in New Jersey in recent years, but one was spotted not long ago in nearby Pennsylvania, perhaps signaling a return of these large creatures. The sandhill crane averages about 12 pounds and is 4 feet long, with an 80-inch wingspread. When in danger, the bird becomes very fierce. These birds have an eerie cry, and participate in a rather striking group mating dance of jumping and hopping. Combined with a penchant for raiding farms for corn, potatoes, and eggs, these attributes could have been interpreted by early settlers as something supernatural.

When it comes to animal theories, there is a wide variety. Gary Giberson, a Port Republic woodcarver whose family has lived on the same land for 14 generations, feels the Jersey Devil noises may, in fact, be the screams of a red fox. Daniel Leeds Mathews, Jr. and William Kunze considered the Jersey Devil to come from owls. They thought that the sharp and eerie cries an owl makes in the woods, combined with the bird's glowing eyes, feed the legend. Earl Danley thinks the shrieks could come from a rabbit after it has been seized by a predator, and Ed Herbert states that packs of wild dogs that roam parts of the Pine Barrens are responsible for acts attributed to the Jersey Devil. Marion Puff, of Sweetwater, offers the theory that the strange Jersey Devil screams heard in the woods are actually the sounds of ice breaking up on the Mullica and other area rivers.

Clyde Birdsall believes vegetation plays a strong role in Jersey Devil lore. He says that at dusk or dawn, people in the Pines can confuse blowing Indian grass, trees, or stumps for the creature. Bill Holton, a forest ranger from Batsto, says that if the Jersey Devil exists, there must be a number of these creatures to sustain a stable population through the years.

The Jersey Devil: Regional Culture, Pride, and Symbolism

For some Jerseyites, the question of the Jersey Devil's existence is secondary to what they call "his significance for the culture of New Jersey." Daniel Rich explained to the authors the spirit of those who are concerned with this aspect of the Jersey Devil's importance: "The Jersey Devil is the foremost and most widely believed bit of local mythology. The Jersey Devil is a slice of the past preserved and constantly renewed by the imagination of Jerseyites. To lose him is to lose a sense of identity and touch with our origins. The Jersey Devil is to us what the Loch Ness Monster is to Scotland. In the face of heightened industrialization and technology, the Jersey Devil is the archetypal fear in us all. The fear of the dark, the unknown and the shaded areas within ourselves."

Linda Reddington, a Manahawkin writer and artist, adds, "Whether the Jersey Devil exists or not is unimportant to me. That the legend exists and is perpetuated is more important. New Jersey, which is rapidly being cemented over and industrialized, needs all the help it can get to preserve a bit of romance and nostalgia."

A folklore researcher, de-emphasizing the question of the Jersey Devil's existence, advocates "the use of the folkloristic method. What interests me is the fact that this legend has enjoyed oral circulation in South Jersey for the last 260 years. The evidence of this oral tale is a fact. Whether or not there was really a Jersey Devil is, in this context, not particularly important. An important question is: How do we account for the longevity of this legend? What functions did this legend serve in South Jersey Piney Folk Culture?"

Two South Jerseyites, Peggy Moran and Lou Rodia, express how personal and interesting the flavor of the Jersey Devil is in New Jersey culture. Peggy Moran, in her article "The Devil Made Me Do It," which appeared in the December 1975 issue of *Philadelphia Magazine*, writes, "I grew up in Medford Lakes. . . when the area was still considered the Pine Barrens. It was then a sparsely-settled resort area, with real log cabins and lakes carved from cranberry bogs. . . .The Jersey Devil was part of my childhood. Free-floating fears of this local evil kept us kids from wandering too far out of our backyards and down those enticing untenanted trails, laced with fairy-tale fern and embroidered all year with Christmas pine cones." And Lou Rodia, who served as Cape May County Publicity Director and who is an outdoor writer, puts his interest this way: "I think that one of my great experiences in life was to sit around campfires as a Boy Scout and have older kids and troop leaders tell us Jersey Devil–type stories."

Those Annoyed By the Legend

Some residents are not particularly happy about the idea of a Jersey Devil. For example, David C. Parris, Assistant Curator of Natural Sciences for the New Jersey State Museum, thought strong interest in the Jersey Devil had caused public apathy concerning the noteworthy phenomenon of dinosaur fossils found in New Jersey: "I am frequently amused at how quickly people bring up the subject of the 'Jersey Devil' when I am asked to identify a fossil (or alleged fossil) from southern New Jersey. Apparently it is not sufficiently remarkable that dinosaurs and mosasaurs once existed in their area; the legendary aspect of a fantastic creature must also be invoked. Journalists are particularly susceptible to the temptation. Apparently the Jersey Devil sells more newspapers than do enormous extinct reptiles."

John Brooms, for years a Chatsworth shopkeeper who had been asked about the beast on countless occasions, told the *Wall Street Journal,* "I've been here for seventy-two years and there's no Jersey Devil. But it might be a good idea to get two or three of them to keep people out." And Nels Clemenson, mayor of Estell Manor City from 1964 to 1976 and owner of the Lazy River Campground, said of the Jersey Devil, "I have a campground and don't want to scare the campers."

What Is Out There?

Of course, there are those who approach the idea of the Jersey Devil with an open mind or a willingness to believe. Tom Brown, author of *The Tracker,* says, "As a white man, I don't believe in it; as a spiritual Indian, I do, and as a tracker, I know anything is possible." Larona Homer, of Vincentown, author of two children's books on New Jersey, often visits schools to read her story, "The Night Simon Saw the Jersey Devil." "Most students," she observes, "are convinced there is a Jersey Devil. Some are doubtful. Very few disbelieve entirely." Richard Andwake, of Blackwood, says, "I believe in the Jersey Devil. I'm always looking for him when I'm in the woods. I'm one of those guys who's ambitious enough to look around for something." And Forked River's Ron F. Stephenson echoes the opinion of believers: "I believe in the Jersey Devil. No one can prove or disprove its existence. I am entitled to my belief: the Jersey Devil is colorful and adds spice to life and has never hurt anyone."

X

THE JERSEY DEVIL AS POP CULTURE

*T*he Jersey Devil legend has been around for so long, it is not surprising he has become part of the popular culture in the area. Teams have been named after him. Clubs, organizations, and businesses have adopted him. He also has been depicted in paintings, sculpture, glass, and poems, and, in fact, his popularity as a symbol or mascot has increased greatly in recent years. The variety of uses the Jersey Devil's name enjoys indicates how well known the legend has become. Additional evidence for the widespread influence of the Jersey Devil on popular culture is provided by Andy Kaff of New York City, the owner of perhaps the most extensive collection of Jersey Devil memorabilia in existence. While spending many summers in Forked River, Kaff developed an interest in the legend and the associated items available to collectors.

Some people object to any commercial or media popularization, arguing that such exploitation detracts from the legend. These purists especially dislike the Jersey Devil's being depicted as a friendly, happy creature, because the older tradition portrays him as diabolic and fierce. Other Jersey Devil fans grow upset when items made in his image are touted as replicas of "their" Jersey Devil.

The Jersey Devil Wins the Stanley Cup

Many teams and organizations, including world championship teams, have taken on the name of the Pine Barrens' famous denizen. The

Madison Campus of Fairleigh Dickinson University adopted the Jersey Devil as its mascot in 1960. The idea originated in an English class, when the professor gave a research assignment on the famous legend. The students were so enthusiastic, the professor suggested to the Director of Physical Health and Education that the Jersey Devil be used as the mascot. The director was impressed with this suggestion, and the Athletic Board adopted the Jersey Devil as the official mascot of the school. Through the years, however, the Jersey Devil logo has changed. Initially, it was a jolly, elf-like creature with bat wings, a forked tail, and horns, who sported a lacrosse stick. The later logo was a map of New Jersey with the phrase "JERSEY DEVILS" printed across it. Their latest mascot is simply "The Devils."

The Jersey Devil has even ascended to the heights of a sports world championship. When the Philadelphia Ramblers, a professional ice hockey team, moved to Cherry Hill, New Jersey, in 1964, they renamed themselves the Jersey Devils. Playing in the Eastern Hockey League, they reached the playoffs in 1966 and 1967, and were disbanded following the 1972–73 season.

But the association of the name with a winning hockey team had only just begun. In 1982, the National Hockey League team of the Colorado Rockies moved to a new home in the Meadowlands Sports Complex in North Jersey. Fans were asked to assist in renaming the team, and the "New Jersey Devils" won out over all the rest! Team owner John McMullen felt the choice was ideal: "We're talking about the Jersey Devil, not any other one. . . I think it's a great name because it combines the folklore of Southern New Jersey with the Meadowlands of Northern New Jersey." And in 1995, the New Jersey Devils won the Stanley Cup.

Another team that used the name is the Jersey Devil Women's Wrestlers—a mud wrestling team. Formed in 1980 in the Lakehurst area by Walt Deetz, their manager, the Jersey Devils consisted of ten women, ranging in age from 19 to 25. Several times a week they performed a program of a dancing show followed by mud wrestling.

The Jersey Devil is well represented in the world of sports. What is now Stone Harbor Country Club, in Cape May Court House, was originally called the Jersey Devil Golf Course. For many years, the Glenn Insurance Company, of Northfield, sponsored the Jersey Devil Tennis

Tournament at Golf and Tennis World, Pleasantville. The oldest continuous car rally in the state of New Jersey, first run in 1957, also boasts the title of the Jersey Devil; one of a series of eight rallies sponsored by the South Jersey Region Sports Car Club of America, the Jersey Devil Rally is held in October and always includes a section of the Pines. The Jersey Devil Dune Buggy Club, founded by Charles Wells in 1978, consisted of 15 members who drove cut-down Volkswagens and appeared in parades, at charity functions, and for general fun. In addition, at one time or another the name of the Jersey Devil has been used for a motorcycle club, a youth soccer team, a country club, a fishing club, a comic book, a skeet shoot, and each year, the Jersey Devil Century Bike Race, sponsored by the South Jersey Wheelmen.

The Jersey Devil on the Water

In the nineteenth century, New Jersey Governor Leon Abbett owned a sailboat dubbed *The Jersey Devil*, and a modern-day sport fishing boat also bore the creature's name. Centered on the stern with

JERSEY DEVIL
ATLANTIC CITY, N.J.

the 46-foot craft proudly bore the image of the Devil holding a rod and reel. Owned by Michael Levitt, the *Jersey Devil* traveled the Atlantic between Canada and the West Indies in search of game fish. A 1,128-pound blue marlin—at one point the world's record—was hauled onto the *Jersey Devil* off Cape Hatteras. Construction of this ship was started in North Carolina in the late 1960s and wasn't completed until 1982. Among the most expensive private fishing boats in the world, this luxurious craft had a custom-made redwood interior, marble inlays, and elaborate electronic equipment.

Other marine associations with the Jersey Devil include a marine supply store in New York's Hudson Valley, a 62-foot *Jersey Devil* fishing boat that books trips out of Barnegat Light, and the Jersey Devil Boat Works, of Lower Bank. This works produces several models, including the Jersey Devil 45-foot Express, starting at $325,000.

Jersey Devil Camps

Logically enough, the Jersey Devil, a creature of the Pines, was taken up by a camping club. Mr. and Mrs. Arba Hudson, of Northfield, founded the Jersey Devil Camping Chapter of the National Campers and Hikers Association in 1963. They camped in Atlantic and Cape May Counties, and the 12 families who composed the group sought to promote better camping. Hudson told the authors that the name was selected because "we have good rapport with the Jersey Devil. He's with us all the way. We're convinced he's done a lot of good and scared a lot of people." Hudson said that when the group was camping, the Jersey Devil would start a campfire for them on command, though no one was standing within 20 to 30 feet of the fire. In May 1978, at Campground #2, Pleasantville, with 125 families looking on, "the Jersey Devil came out of the woods and started the fire." This Jersey Devil bore a striking resemblance to Arba Hudson.

The Jersey Devil in Business

The Jersey Devil's name shows up in business, too. *The Jersey Devil,* a monthly newspaper, was founded in 1975, in New Egypt, New Jersey. *The Jersey Devil's Official Flea Marketeer's Manual* contained monthly features articles and listings of flea and farmers' markets, auctions, antiques, shops, and the like.

An architectural design group calling itself Jersey Devil is based in New Jersey, but it has undertaken projects throughout the country. The company consists of four builders/designers who advocate a style of construction that blends into the natural setting—something the Jersey Devil has done for years. This company's accomplishments have been written up in such publications as the *New York Times* and *Popular Science*.

Jersey Devils Inc., a contracting company that specializes in decks, pilings, and bulkheads, is headquartered across the bay from the creature's Leeds Point birthplace, in Brigantine. The Jersey Devil also added its name to a souvenir store in Ocean City. Clearly enough, the name of the Jersey Devil lends a popular, unique local flair to a business.

About twenty years ago, Richard Andwake opened his shop, Jersey

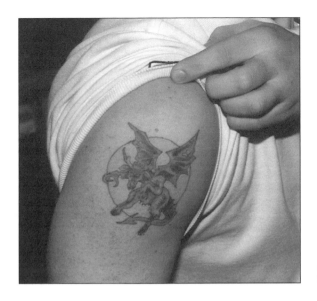

A Jersey Devil tattoo.
Ray Miller, photographer

Devil's Tattooing, in Blackwood, New Jersey. Andwake selected the name because of his ongoing interest in the Jersey Devil. Of the 800 general devil designs Mr. Andwake rendered since opening his shop, about 25 were called Jersey Devil tattoos. Now in other hands, the store also features Jersey Devil t-shirts, and its walls are adorned with pictures of the Pine Barrens' famous demon.

The Jersey Devil even worked his way into the baking business. The D.D.D. Baking Company, of Sea Isle City, New Jersey, distributed a small snack cake that they called "Mom's Jersey Devil."

Not only have a number of businesses taken the Jersey Devil's name as their formal title, the Devil has also became a nickname or logo. Most notably, the 177th Fighter Interceptor Group of the New Jersey Air National Guard, based in the Pines outside of Atlantic City, took the Jersey Devil as their mascot in the mid-1950s, and have kept him since. Lieutenant Michael E. Deibert, of the "Jersey Devils," reported to the authors, "The name was chosen because of our unity with our area and history." Subsequent to adopting the Jersey Devil, the 177th sported a bright red patch with the head of the Jersey Devil emblazoned on it, and they decorated their planes with a bright Jersey Devil logo. Unfortunately, the logo on the planes was replaced by a New Jersey Air National Guard logo: In the words of Lieutenant Deibert, "The main complaint about our Jersey Devil logo is that it looked too much like a dead steer!"

Several CB operators who drive along Delaware Valley roads use the handle "The Jersey Devil," and Herb Leeds, of Leeds Point, has been dubbed "The Jersey Devil Woodcarver," because of his avocation of wildlife carving. Less illustriously, Willie Borton, a burglar of the 1930s, was known to various police departments as "The Jersey Devil."

Stamps, Floats, and Singers

It is amazing to note the degree to which the Jersey Devil has worked his way into the popular culture of the region. He even was nominated for a stamp. In August 1966, Ethel Noyes, who with her husband, Fred, operated the Smithville Inn at the time, suggested that the Jersey Devil's image be placed on a postage stamp for the American Folklore series. The proposal was received by the Citizens' Advisory Committee on Postage Stamps, but, unfortunately, it was not approved. In 1978, the Miss America Pageant parade in Atlantic City included a Jersey Devil float, and the banner of the Woodstown Rotary Club uses as its emblem a vivid picture of the Jersey Devil. In 1970, a Jersey Devil Barbershop Quartet was formed as part of the Pine Barrens Chorus, and Bosh Pritchard, its lead singer, had been a running back with the World Champion Philadelphia Eagles in 1949.

Drawings, Pictures, and Posters

A number of drawings and posters portray the Jersey Devil. Portraits by Linda Reddington and Ed Sheetz are among the most well known. Reddington's Devils, which appear on various media including t-shirts, are on the frightening side: horns; huge, powerful wings; a long, thick reptilian tail; scaly skin; and long, fierce nails. Sheetz's sketches of the Jersey Devil, on posters, postcards, and other objects, may have added to the frequent conception of the Jersey Devil as a more friendly and playful creature through their popularity. One of his widely circulated renditions shows the Jersey Devil standing in the Pines. He is a small creature with cat-like hindquarters, a pointed head, small horns, a puckish smile on his face, and wearing a small vest.

E.A. Brinckhoff made an interesting woodcut, entitled "The Jersey Devil Draws a Beer." It depicts an early American scene, with an anthropoid Jersey Devil dressed in late eighteenth-century human garb, tapping a keg and filling a tankard. Pat Hillman, of Seaville, did a woodburning on an eight-inch wooden plate of the Jersey Devil. This creature has cloven hooves, a human body, wings and horns, and is sporting a smile.

Geni Alles' natural wood art version of the famous monster was done in the early 1970s. Alles, who resides in Bargaintown, noted that the piece of wood from which she carved the Jersey Devil's face had naturally seemed to form some vague head of a strange creature, and her design only amplified the weird nature of this head.

Renard Wiseman, of New Gretna, took a photograph that some people claim actually shows the Jersey Devil. In July 1978, Wiseman was involved in combating a wave of forest fires sweeping the Pines, and he escorted a newspaper photographer into the forest. Both men took a number of pictures. When Wiseman's photographs were developed, he noticed something definitely out of the ordinary in one of the shots. Somewhere in the mass of flaming trees, a barely discernible outline of a figure can be seen. Word spread that the Jersey Devil had been captured—if only on film. Wiseman stated that the CIA had examined the photograph for authenticity and found no sign of retouching.

Colonel Howard Benge, a retired Marine from Ocean City, carved a two-foot-high statue of the Jersey Devil in 1978. It resembles the small imp in the Ed Sheetz drawings. Benge presented the carving to William McMahon, the well-known South Jersey writer and journalist, who showed the carving one night when he was delivering a speech on South Jersey history. One woman in the audience gasped audibly. After the speech, she told McMahon that she and her husband had seen a Devil that looked just like the carving running through the Pines in Burlington County. Her husband, who was also in the audience, refused to go near the statue.

At the Festival

Since 1976, the Jersey Devil has been the logo of the New Jersey Folk Festival. Each year, the Devil is pictured in a slightly different manner as the symbol of this event held at Douglass College of Rutgers University in New Brunswick. One year, the Devil was shown riding a hot air balloon, and during another, he was depicted playing a fiddle. Founded by Dr. Angus Gillespie, of the American Studies Department of Douglass College, the Festival provides a major forum for viewing the whole spectrum of New Jersey folklore.

The Jersey Devil in Glass

In a state long known for its glass production, it was inevitable the Jersey Devil would be represented in this art form. Around 1920, the F.S. Reed's Sons Apothecary, of Atlantic City, started distributing some of their medicines in a "Jersey Devil Medicine Bottle," which they probably had manufactured in Millville. With its decorative top, the milk-glass bottle stood six inches tall, and it portrayed a winged creature with hooved forelegs; a scaly body with a long, fish-like tail; and a massive head with a forked tongue. C.F. Kier of Oak Towne owned one of the few still in existence.

The Jersey Devil also appeared on a 1974 bottle, issued by the Holly City Bottle Company of Millville, New Jersey. The green, eight-inch-tall bottle sported a traditional, Beelzebub-type devil, with horns,

The Jersey Devil in glass, by Michael Dorofee. Photography by Susan Miller

spiked beard, bat wings, animal legs, split hooves, pointed tail—menacingly smiling as he wields a pitchfork in this limited edition of 1000. According to Ed Johnson of Holly City Bottle, "The Jersey Devil himself was consulted when we did the design work for the bottle." If another edition should appear, Johnson says, it will be a different shape and color—no doubt according to the wishes of the Jersey Devil himself.

On Route 9, between New Gretna and Tuckerton, Michael Dorofee, of Dorofee's Glass Works, produces a unique Jersey Devil. Over the years, the talented Dorofee has created several hundred Jersey Devils in his diminutive workshop, deep in the heart of Jersey Devil country, where the pines and the salt marshes begin to merge. Dorofee turns out a variety of glass items, including small Jersey Devil Christmas tree ornaments and Jersey Devil swizzle sticks. The Devil, in figurines of many sizes, is among the most popular of his works. While most of Dorofee's customers seem happy with their Jersey Devils, one Tuckerton woman claimed that her glass Jersey Devil brought her bad luck—so she smashed it.

Poems, Songs, and Plays

Through the years, the Jersey Devil has inspired poetry and verse to memorialize his exploits. A view of selected Jersey Devil poems shows a variety of meters and approaches by the poets, once again demonstrating the rich imagery of the Jersey Devil in popular culture.

Linda Reddington, a writer and artist from Manahawkin, deals primarily with the creature's birth in her poem "The Jersey Devil." The lines of the poem, predominantly in four-foot balladlike meter, have end rhyme and catch the dramatic mood and atmosphere of the event. This is probably the most widely circulated contemporary poem on the legend.

Lilli Lopez's poem "Hey, Mother Leeds—The Midwife's Lament" is a sprightly lyric, rendered in dialect, involving a narrator who is supposedly Mother Leeds' midwife. The poem appears in Mrs. Lopez's collection of poems, *Story Poems of the Coastal Pinelands*.

A brief, humorous lyric that describes the diabolic atmosphere around Leeds Point was written by Dr. Andrea Lippi, of Goshen. "Leeds Devil" is a short line poem that lightly warns the reader to

Jersey Devil performer Cliff Oakley makes many appearances every year at parties and other social events. Cornelius Hogenbirk, photographer

watch out around Leeds Point. Lippi also drew an accompanying picture. He has distributed copies of this illustrated lyric as far away as Spain.

A ballad by Emma Van Sant Moore, "The Leeds' Devil," appeared in her book of poetry, *The Mullica,* and Jack "Mud Whomp" Stackhouse, whose roots are in the coastal Pine Barrens area, turned out "A Devil of a Tale" while standing long night watches in the U.S. Navy. The ballad is based on stories he heard as a child.

The famous week in 1909 also inspired an award-winning ballad by Leah Bodine Drake, "The Ballad of the Jabberwock." Winner of the Stephen Vincent Benet ballad contest in 1946, it has since been reprinted in various anthologies, such as *A Hornbook for Witches,* by Leah Bodine Drake, and *Dark of the Moon,* edited by August Derleth. The town in the subtitle, Squankom Town, is an archaic name for Williamstown (which by 1909 was already called by its current name), and means "place of the evil god." This very strong, imaginative ballad deals with Jersey Devil sightings (the "Jabberwock" of the title) in Williamstown during 1909.

The Jersey Devil has inspired dramatists as well. Jim Albertson, of Mauricetown, New Jersey, folklorist and entertainer, includes Jersey Devil material in his performances. In 1976, *The Scourge,* a play about the Jersey Devil written by Bill Mastrisimore and directed by Margaret Dawson, was presented at the New Jersey Folk Festival, providing a sympathetic treatment of the gypsy curse version of the devil's birth.

Jersey Devil Costume Tales

Pat Oleszko, a New York costume designer and performer, was commissioned by *Oui* magazine to design and model a Jersey Devil costume for an article on monsters in the United States in the August 1973 issue. Oleszko and the photographers headed to New Jersey, stopping at a Howard Johnson's restaurant that was near some pine trees. While the photographers drank coffee, Oleszko went into the women's room to change into the costume. When she emerged from the women's room, walked out the door, and stood under the pines for the photographers, the restaurant customers were amused—but startled—to see the Jersey Devil at Howard Johnson's.

Drink to the Jersey Devil's Health

The Jersey Devil has also influenced drinking habits in South Jersey. A number of libations are named after him, but the most famous Jersey Devil cocktail was concocted by Ethel and Fred Noyes, of the Smithville Inn, which was near Leeds Point. This is their recipe, which they served in a special Jersey Devil glass:

1 1/2 ounces Laird's Apple Jack Brandy
1 ounce Cointreau
1 ounce lemon juice
3 ounces cranberry juice
2 shakes of Frothee

Shake well with ice, and pour into an 8 1/2-ounce glass.

Some cranberry growers in Ocean County claim they were the first to invent a Jersey Devil cocktail, and Ocean Spray Cranberries, Inc., offers two different recipes:

JERSEY DEVIL PUNCH 1

1 1/2   quarts Apple Jack
1 quart Ocean Spray Cranberry Juice cocktail, chilled
1/3   quart Triple Sec
1/2   quart lemon juice

Combine ingredients, stir well, and serve over ice. Serves 4 to 8.

JERSEY DEVIL PUNCH 2

2 ounces Apple Jack
1/3   jigger Cointreau
1/3   jigger lime juice
1/3   jigger Ocean Spray Cranberry Juice cocktail, chilled
1/2 teaspoon sugar

Combine ingredients, stir well, and serve over ice.

The cranberry juice in all these drinks comes from South Jersey's famous cranberries, one of the few crops that thrives in the soil of the Pine Barrens.

Bill Thompson, who has spent a lot of time in the Pines, claims the following is the most potent of all the Jersey Devil drinks. Thompson warns it should be drunk very slowly, however, and in concert with a sufficient amount of food:

2 ounces Apple Jack
2 ounces hard cider
1 dash of cranberry juice (for coloring only)

Thompson guarantees that finishing this drink will cause an appearance of the Jersey Devil.

Sometimes, people swear the Jersey Devil appears to those who engage in drinking other libations as well. In the summer of 1975, in Bricktown, a group of people were sitting around, drinking, when they saw what they said was an "old, troll-like man running down the road." All the members of this group quickly agreed that it was the Jersey Devil.

A Vineland man also reported an incident from 1960: "A friend and I were driving from Vineland to Atlantic City, when an old black Plymouth shot by us. We couldn't see anything inside the car except a glowing red color. It was very bright. We saw the car turn up a sand road and followed it. The car and its tracks suddenly disappeared. What else could it have been but the Jersey Devil? Of course we were drinking at the time—but not that much."

Another slightly inebriated Vineland man placed a sombrero on his head, sat in the middle of the street, and proclaimed he was the Jersey Devil.

XI

IN SEARCH OF
THE JERSEY DEVIL

*P*eople often ask how we, the authors, became interested in the Jersey Devil and how we collect our information. Both of us were born and raised in New Jersey, and we frequently heard stories over the years. Interestingly enough, it was not until we were both in Delaware that we began comparing notes on this famous phenomenon of New Jersey and started actively pursuing stories and information about the legend. This eventually led to publication of *The Jersey Devil* in 1976 (and to subsequent printings). Because of the book and our continuing pursuit of the legend, more and more stories, material, and contacts kept developing. Over the years, we came to feel the growing interest in this unique folk phenomenon, plus the plethora of research we had collected, warranted another book.

One of the most rewarding facets of researching the Jersey Devil is meeting people and hearing their stories. The many deeply interesting people of South Jersey we have worked with through the years have made this book possible by sharing their experiences in rich and entertaining detail.

We have met our informants in a variety of ways. Outside of Hammonton, on the road to Batsto, we stopped to photograph a bus stop advertising the New Gretna House—specifically, its Jersey Devil taproom. Our Delaware license plate and camera drew Anthony De-

Marco's attention. When we explained we were gathering information on the Jersey Devil, he told us his wife's aunt had seen the creature, and he directed us to Bessie LoSasso's house. We spent several hospitable hours sipping coffee while Mrs. LoSasso shared her Devil tales.

One sunny August day in the late 1970s, one of the authors chanced upon an elderly man selling salt hay by the side of the road in Barnegat. Andrew Broom, born in 1896, recalled that in 1917 and 1920, people were running through the streets of Barnegat, frightened and crying out that the Jersey Devil was pursuing them. And while on a vacation in Ship Bottom in 1980, one of the authors picked up a copy of *Shoreline Guide 1980,* by William Kunze, whose fascinating account of the legend led to a visit to his house, where more Jersey Devil lore was garnered.

Even car trouble proved serendipitous. Late one summer night, as we were driving home from the Ocean County Park's Jersey Devil

Authors James F. McCloy and Ray Miller, Jr. examine a brick from one of the reported Jersey Devil Leeds Point birthsites. Photography by Susan Miller

night walk, the car broke down outside of Malaga. We were beginning to wonder whether the Jersey Devil himself might visit us on this relatively remote stretch of road in the middle of the night, when instead we made the acquaintance of Trooper John DeFeo, of the New Jersey State Police, who not only assisted us with our car, but also offered interesting bits of lore he had heard which we have included in this book.

Knowing that Robert Kuppell's property encompassed the ruins of several supposed birthsites of the Jersey Devil at Leeds Point, we paid him a visit. It was a boiling hot day, but Mr. Kuppell graciously led us down the sandy road. Bedeviled by the swarming attacks of legions of strawberry flies, we followed him into the woods, which were thickly crowded with poison ivy, brush, cedar, and pines, to observe the infamous areas, now little more than vine-covered foundations in the sandy soil of Leeds Point.

While we were spotting sites at Atsion for a television interview on the Jersey Devil, we encountered Robert Gaskill, a New Jersey forest ranger, who descibed the incident of the two campers in 1978. Earl Danley, a ranger in Lebanon State Forest, provided us with Jersey Devil lore when we were researching the famous demon in that vicinity, and another ranger there remembered a Jersey Devil incident in New Egypt around 1966–67. This helpful lead sent us to Edward Early, who was the police chief there at the time.

A review of *The Jersey Devil* by Edward McFadden appeared in the *Journal of American Folklore* in the late 1970s and contained a citation of an article by Gordon R. Strasenburgh in *Northwest Anthropological Notes,* which we obtained from Boise State University. This article not only directed us to a very striking article in the *New York Times* of 1927, which told of a posse in Bridgeport, New Jersey, but also led us to Anne Waters, editor and publisher of the *Swedesboro News.*

In searching for the Jersey Devil, we have spent many hours poring over old newspapers, records, and documents. The constant flow of letters and correspondence sent from other writers and some very nice clippings received from friends and those who had read our first book also swelled our databank on the legend. Extensive phone conversations with a wide variety of informants have kept the Devil discussions flowing.

The Jersey Devil Dune Buggy Club once appeared briefly in the

Philadelphia Mummers Parade. We traced them with the help of the Mummers Museum. The Jersey Devil Women's Mud Wrestlers came to our attention through a radio commercial about their next appearance. Finding the Jersey Devil Tattoo Parlor was another random piece of luck. While driving down the Black Horse Pike through Blackwood, one of the authors spotted the words "Jersey Devil Tattooing" out of the corner of his eye.

The search for Jersey Devil stories and lore is virtually endless. There are still many stories, both oral and written, waiting to be told, out there.

THE JERSEY DEVIL
Linda Reddington

She cursed the day she and Leeds were wed
   Heavy with life she held her head
and cried to the midwife, silent and grim,
   "Twelve children I have given him!
Still young, I am old, pale, and sick with wear.
   Twelve hungry mouths, twelve burdens to bear!
Fair I was, and strong, when the banns were read,
   all pink of cheek with flaxen head,
sparkling of eye and silken of limb,
   but I had to go and marry him!
What would I give to escape his life—
   to have done with pain, to be no man's wife,
no children to tend to, no chores to be done,
   to have youth and beauty, to have some fun!
Oh what I could give to end this birth,
   this horrible weight, this obscene girth!
I'd like to bear the Devil's child—
   all claw and fang, all fierce and wild—
Such sweet revenge to see Leeds' face

when he finds a beast in the baby's place!"
The wood fire leaped and began to crackle,
   the room was filled with a demon cackle,
the woman screamed, then the quiet returned.
   In the dim, still room her pale eyes burned.
She shivered and shook with fear and dread.
   "I didn't mean it, those things I said!"
"Hush, my dear," the midwife said,
   "Your labor's begun, best go to bed."
The woman writhed on her dank, soiled cot.
   The fire blazed and the room grew hot.
It bathed the walls in a hellish red.
   The midwife swabbed her damp forehead
and drew the child from his mother's womb.
   A hideous shriek ripped through the room.
A claw shot and scratched the cheek
   of the midwife, now too numb to speak.
It slashed and tore and left her dead.
   Then turned, and lifting its horse-like head,
gave a sanguine smile to its mother there,
   a giggling idiot, twisting her hair,
her youth regained but to no avail.
   It stroked her face with its serpentine-tail,
gave a practising shrug of each leathery wing,
   then flew up the chimney in one great spring.
Now it prowls the pines in the damp of night,
   when a gibbous moon spends its sickly light.
A child of darkness, who leaves in the sand
   a cloven hoofprint, the mark of a hand,
a broken branch, or a claw…who knows?
   But the wise pinewoodsman never goes
alone in the Barrens late at night.
   He fears the blue heron in its flight;
avoids the red orchid, passes it by,
   leaves it to suckle the carrion fly;
starts at the sudden crack of a twig.
   Something is moving there—something big!
There are charms to be carried. Don't tempt the fates.
   The Jersey Devil watches and waits!

HEY, MOTHER LEEDS
Lilli Lopez

The night, it was stormy—the hour was late,
We brought forth the Leeds' babe for a life doomed for hate.

Hey, Mother Leeds, yer little one's here,
Lookit that tiny face—ain't he a dear?
I know, Mother Leeds, you say thirteen's a curse,
But he has his needs—take him to nurse.
Please don't ignore him—he's just the same,
As those come before him—O give him a name.

But all of our pleddin' fell on her deaf ear,
As she pushed him and screamed, we shivered with fear.

Hey, Mother Leeds, you know its yer place
To hold him awhile—kiss his tormented face.
O see how he's growin'—where'd he git that tail?
Watch how he changes—O hear his poor wail.
There he goes up the chimney—don't it chill yer soul,
For that pitiful chile to take on such a role?

This forenoon me 'n' Sophie walked across town,
To see if there's truth in the tales goin' roun'.

Hey, Mother Leeds, don't you dare shet that door.
We'es heard them talkin' down in the store.
Strange things is hap'nin—don't you wonder why
Henhouses been robbed and cows is gone dry?
They're sayin' its yer chile—now ain't you ashame?
Poor tortured younggun, and jes you to blame.

Hey, Mother Leeds, yer poor tormented child
Is flyin' on bat's wings up there in the wile.
When you hear the dogs braying y'ell know, Mother Leeds,
He's aroun and yer fambly will grieve for his deeds.
But he'll bear the brunt of that witch spell you gave,
And he'll haunt you until you are deep in yer grave.

From *Story Poems of the Coastal Pinelands* by Lilli Lopez. Reprinted with permission from the author.

THE BALLAD OF THE JABBERWOCK
(A True Tale of Squankom Town)
Leah Bodine Drake

My grandmother tells me,
  When the lights are low,
How the Jabberwock appeared
  In Squankom long ago.

First a frightened farmer,
  Tearing into town,
Told how his wife had seen
  Something big and brown,

Horned like a billy goat
  And scaled like a dragon,
Perched cross-legged on
  Their brand-new wagon.

It leaped into the barn
  And hid in the hay.
She screeched blue murder
  And fainted away!

The Timmermans saw It,
  Coming from Cross Keys;
It crept from Corkray's Wood
  And peered 'round the trees.

Footprints were found in fields
  Clawed like a bird's;
It clumped over Karsh's roof
  Gibbering words.

Then folks began to see It
  Here and everywhere.
Clinging to the steeple,
  Winging through the air

From *A Hornbook for Witches* (Poems of Fantasy) by Leah Bodine Drake. Reprinted with permission from the publisher, Arkham House.

With fans of a mighty bat;
  Or walking in a pasture
Upright as any man
  And cocky as a master!

Squankom locked all its doors
  And bright lamps were lit
In chilly front parlors
  Where folks seldom sit.

Except for a funeral
  Or the minister's call.
But what lurks in darkness
  They lighted up all.

Some few were skeptical
  And would only smile;
But the path to the barn at night
  Seemed like a mile!

Reverend Walsey preached of sin,
  And most folks agreed
That It was a warning
  They had better heed.

They named It *The Jabberwock*
  For want of another;
But some shook their heads: "It's
  The Devil's own brother!"

Then people came to church
  Who'd never been yet.
Some patched up a quarrel
  And some paid a debt.

Cousin Flo and Cousin Kate
  Forgot they didn't speak;
And Old Man Jones stayed sober
  For one amazing week.

Wives left off nagging
  And husbands kissed their wives.
The Claybrook brothers went to work
  For once in their lives.

No one watered any milk
  Or cut the measures down;
And Tillie got religion
  And all her girls left town!

Then one day the town awoke
  To find It had fled:
No one saw It squatting
  On his barn or shed.

No one saw those footprints
  Huge upon his lawn....
Suddenly, as It had come,
  The Jabberwock had gone.

The church held a meeting,
  And great thanks were given
That Satan had done his worst
  And left them scared but shriven.

Satan had ramped about
  Like a roaring lion;
But Squankom held firm, and now
  Was a little Zion.

They were the wonder-town
  Of the countryside!
They had driven Evil out!
  They let Good abide

For almost a fortnight....
  Then someone stole a sack
Of flour out of Barker's store,
  And Tillie's girls came back.

UNTITLED

Oh the Devil's loose in Bucks and the
  Folks have seen his track,
They're keeping up their courage now
  With jogs of applejack.
And prowling round at night they see
  Those awful red eyed things,
That sit upon a roof and crow and
  Flap their greenish wings.

Oh little children, keep you close,
  Don't go outside the house,
This awful thing will get you—It is
  Called the Dinglewoose
It lives in jugs and barrels and it
  Leaves a hoof-like track,
And you can see it plainer when
  You're full of applejack.

From the *Bucks County Republican*, January 22, 1909.

THAT WOZZLE BIRD
W.S.F.

Now all you little children who on
   the streets would roam,
Instead of going straight to school, directly from your home,
I warn you to be careful and never
   'tempt to play
Truant, or perhaps, very, very, soon
   you may—
Run right into it—then I know you'll
   cry and shout
For the "Wozzle Bird" will git yer if
   yer don't watch out.

Now you people in the country living
   near to Broad Street Park,
Should keep yer eyes a squintin' and
   listen for a bark,
And don't undertake to open the barn
   or woodshed door,
'Thout kinder peepin' through the knot-
   hole just before
You do do, or if you don't,
   no doubt
The "Wozzle Bird" will git yer if you
   don't watch out.

Now you banqueters in the city who
   stay out late at night,
And though you do not mean it, get a
   little more than "right,"
And stay out in the morning, perhaps
   till one or two,
Then start and ramble 't'ward your
   home, where wife awaits for you,
Of course you do not fear her because
   you are big and stout,
But if that "Wozzle Bird" should git
   you, then don't watch out.

From the *Daily State Gazette*, Trenton, N.J., January 23, 1909.

THE JERSEY DEVIL

The Jabberwock or the Hickapoo—
    Built on the plans of a kangaroo;
Covered with leather and eyes that
    glow—
    Breathes fire from its nostrils,
And stalks through the snow;
    Has hoofs like a pony,
Though it flies through the air,
    But no one seems able
    To locate its lair.

From the *Morning News*, Wilmington, Del., January 24, 1909.

CHRONOLOGY

SURVEY OF SOME JERSEY DEVIL INCIDENTS

1730	Mount Holly	Benjamin Franklin reports a witchcraft trial, which some believe could have influenced the origin of the legend *(Pennsylvania Gazette)*.
1735		This is the most common year given as the birthdate of the Jersey Devil.
1740	Pine Barrens	Clergyman exorcises Jersey Devil with bell, book, and candle for 100 years.
1776	Salem, Gloucester, Cumberland Counties	The Jersey Devil is seen before the Revolutionary War.
1790 (October)	Near present-day Lebanon State Forest	Vance Larner describes his encounter with a strange, Jersey Devil–like creature, and records the incident in his diary, although he does not use the words "Jersey Devil."
1803	Hanover Iron Works	Commodore Stephen Decatur, according to the legend, drills a cannonball through the middle of the Jersey Devil, with apparently little effect.
1810(?)	New Brunswick	A farmer observes a "winged deer" devouring wild berries and leaves.
1816–39	Pine Barrens	Joseph Bonaparte, former king of Spain and brother of Napoleon, observes the Jersey Devil while hunting in the Pine Barrens. (Bonaparte lived in Bordentown during these years.)

1835	Pine Barrens	The Jersey Devil's cries are louder than usual this year, constantly disturbing residents.
1840	Pine Barrens	The Jersey Devil rampages through the area, eating livestock.
1846	Cape May County	Shortly before the outbreak of the Mexican War, the Jersey Devil is seen flying about.
1858	Hanover Iron Works	W.F. Mayer, in an 1859 article in *Atlantic Monthly*, reported fear of the Leeds Devil among certain residents during this year.
1859	Haddonfield	The Jersey Devil is seen in town.
1860–61	Jersey Coast	The Jersey Devil is seen flying up and down the coast, warning people of the coming Civil War.
1868 (January–February)	Gloucester County	Jersey Devil footprints are observed in Mullica Hill and surrounding areas.
1870	Atlantic Ocean	The Jersey Devil is seen swimming with a mermaid.
1872 or 1873	Conovertown	Daniel Conover shoots at the Jersey Devil.
1873–74	Bridgeton	The Jersey Devil prowls the area during these years.
1874	Osbornville	Tony Hulse encounters the Jersey Devil twice.
1880s	Pine Barrens	The Jersey Devil attacks an unusually large number of livestock.
1884 (January)	Atlantic City	Heavy storms that batter the coast are attributed by some residents to an angered Jersey Devil.
1890	Absecon	The Jersey Devil is seen prowling about the vicinity.
1894	Smithville Long Beach Island Brigantine Beach Leeds Point Haddonfield	These locations are visited by the Jersey Devil.
1898	Monmouth and Atlantic Counties	The Jersey Devil is seen before the Spanish-American War.
1899	Vincentown Burrsville	The Jersey Devil is sighted in these locations.
1899	Spring Valley, NY	George Saarosy hears ungodly screams and sees a flying serpent.

1901		Folklorist Charles Skinner writes in *American Myths and Legends* that the Jersey Devil will soon be forgotten.
1909 (January)	Countless locations in New Jersey, Pennsylvania, and Delaware	This is the most famous week in the Jersey Devil's long history, during which he appears at hundreds of locations.
1913	Glassboro	Footprints of the Jersey Devil are seen in town.
1915	Chatsworth	Bessie LoSasso and others are frightened after encountering the Jersey Devil in the woods.
1917	Paterson	A strange animal of some type, reported to be the Jersey Devil, is killed and put on display.
1917 1920	Barnegat	People flee up and down the streets, saying they were chased by the Jersey Devil, which resembled a horse.
1920s	Salem	A posse drives the Jersey Devil up a tree, but he escapes.
1920s	West Orange	A posse pursues a "flying lion" and claims to have captured one of its cubs.
1925	Greenwich Township	William Hyman claims to have killed the Jersey Devil. Later searches find no record of a man by that name in the area.
1925	Swedesboro	The Jersey Devil's "body" is found in a tree.
1927	Bridgeport	Frank Ryder leads a posse in search of the Jersey Devil, which is described as being quick, and the size of a fox, with feathers.
1927	Salem	A taxi driver encounters a large, hairy beast while changing a flat tire.
1928	Batsto	Not far from here, William Bozarth encounters the Jersey Devil along the Mullica River one night. The Jersey Devil approaches him, then flees into the woods.
1929 (December)	Philadelphia, PA	Norman Jefferies admits his part in a 1909 hoax, in which he dressed a kangaroo in the guise of the Jersey Devil. He mistakenly gives the year of the hoax as 1906.
1930	Leeds Point Mays Landing	Berry pickers in both locations encounter the Jersey Devil.
1930	Erial	Howard Marcey and John Huntzinger see the Jersey Devil blasting the tops off trees.
1930(?)	Great Meadows	A vigilante committee is formed following reports that the Jersey Devil is in the area.

1930 (July)	Mays Landing	The Jersey Devil is seen by a number of people.
1932 (January)	Lindell, PA	Excitement is created in the area after the Jersey Devil appears, and some residents react by arming themselves.
1934		Willie Borton, accused criminal, takes the nickname "The Jersey Devil."
1934	Iona Lake	A number of people investigate what are reported to be Jersey Devil footprints.
1935	Woodstown	Philip Smith observes the Jersey Devil, which he says looks something like a German Shepherd, walking down the street.
1935 (October)	Absecon	The Jersey Devil creates a series of horrible cries in the pines and marshes.
1936	Woodstown	A heavily armed posse roams the woods and fields in pursuit of the Jersey Devil. They hear screams and cries.
1936	Batsto	William Bozarth sees the Jersey Devil again.
1937 (May)	Lakehurst	Before the crash of the *Hindenburg*, the Jersey Devil is seen by a number of local residents, who later view this appearance as a premonition of the disaster.
1937 (July)	Dorlan/ Milford Mills, PA	Three people see a hairy, kangaroo-like beast.
1930s (late)	Leeds Point	The area experiences a rash of Jersey Devil sightings, and numerous footprints are found.
1930s (late)	Lower Bank	During full moons, the Jersey Devil is often heard clomping across the Lower Bank bridge.
1930s (late)	South Jersey	The Jersey Devil is reported to be giving out food to those in need during this period of the Depression.
1930s (late)	Sewell	When a prehistoric fossil is unearthed, some people nickname it "the first Jersey Devil."
1939		*New Jersey: A Guide to its Past and Present* unofficially proclaims the Jersey Devil the official state demon.
1940	Somerville	A green, male monster is seen in the area.
1941	Vancouver, British Columbia	A strange, sea serpent–like creature, with a horse-like head and bulbous nose, washes ashore. Some people announce this is the carcass of the Jersey Devil.
1941 (December 7)	Mount Holly	The Jersey Devil is seen here on Pearl Harbor Day.

1944	Trenton	Walter Edge, who served as governor of New Jersey, United States senator, and ambassador to France, says that he felt threatened by the Jersey Devil as a child.
1944 (July)	Rancocas Woods	Some people claim the Jersey Devil is in the area. After a wild hog is shot, some persist in claiming that the Jersey Devil is still at large.
1945 (November)	North Coventry Township, PA	Many people arm themselves in both official and unofficial posses in searches for the Jersey Devil.
1948 (October)	Mount Holly	A number of area residents board their doors and remain on alert following a rumor that the Jersey Devil is due to appear in town.
1951 (November)	Gibbstown	Appearances by the Jersey Devil and claims of hearing his screams draw crowds of thrill-seekers to the area. Police must calm children and contend with traffic jams.
1952	Whitesbog	Mysterious footprints turn out to be the work of a prankster with a bear's foot on a pole.
1952	Batsto	The Jersey Devil again prowls one of his favorite locations.
1952	Upper Freehold Township	The Jersey Devil is prowling in this area.
1955 (July)	Jackson Mills	The Jersey Devil is heard screaming in the woods, and leaves his footprints there.
1957 (October)	Hampton Furnace	Charred bones, claws, and feathers are found in the debris of an earlier forest fire, and some again claim the demise of the Jersey Devil.
1960	Dorothy	Strange screams are heard in the pines, and game wardens set out traps.
1963	Atsion	Five men on a Jersey Devil hunt hear weird screams and find mysterious footprints.
1965	Glassboro Fish & Wildlife Management Area	Police shoot at strange noises from some creature in the woods.
1965	Green Bank Weekstown	Jersey Devil screams are heard in the woods for several nights in a row.
1965	Harvey Cedars	Mysterious sounds heard out at sea are attributed by some to the Jersey Devil.
1965 (December)	Leeds Point	Robert Nisky and a relative hear a loud scream coming from one of the houses reputed to be the birthplace of the Jersey Devil.

1966 (April)	Marigold Branch, Mullica River	The farm of Stephen Silkotch is ravaged by what some say is the Jersey Devil. Thirty-one ducks, three geese, four cats, and two large dogs are lost.
1966 (summer)	Plumstead Township	A family sleeps with baseball bats after seeing what they claim was the Jersey Devil in their backyard.
1966	Washington, D.C.	The U.S. Postal Service receives a proposal to put the Jersey Devil on a postage stamp.
1967 (summer)	Plumstead Township	After a Jersey Devil sighting, a number of teenagers in North Hanover Township will not venture out at night.
1968	Green Bank	A strange creature is seen and heard in a blueberry field.
1968–70	Howell Township	Billy Dunnkosky experiences a number of encounters with the Jersey Devil, which comes onto his property. Once, he is even able to shoot at the creature.
1969	Sweetwater	Bill Kronmayer witnesses the Jersey Devil jump across the road in front of his car.
1970s	Mercer County	A young woman says that a "creature" pulled the hair out of her child's head.
1971	Leeds Point	The Jersey Devil is blamed for the death of a number of chickens.
1973 (March)	Upper Pottsgrove Township, PA	A huge, cat-like creature, suspected by some of being the Jersey Devil, reportedly kills chickens and rabbits.
1974 (fall)	Reed's Bay, off Brigantine	Howard Mosley sees a weird, kangaroo- and goat-like creature near the shoreline, hopping about.
1975 (August)	Williamstown	A horse is found with its throat torn out. Some believe this is the work of the Jersey Devil.
1976 (early)	Southern Texas	Huge "Big Birds" are observed in a number of locations by different witnesses. This leads to a "move" by some to return the Jersey Devil to its home state.
1976 (summer)	Jackson Mills	A service station attendant states that the Jersey Devil follows him home every night.
1976 (November)	Pedricktown	The mysterious, sometimes violent deaths of pigs on several farms here is suspected by some of being the work of the Jersey Devil.
1977 (January)	Chatsworth	The Jersey Devil is seen here.

1977 (July)	Pine Barrens	A woman claims that the Jersey Devil was eating her blueberries as she left them in boxes throughout the field.
1977 (summer)	Penns Grove	A large, hairy beast seizes the door handle of a woman's car and is able to run alongside the car at a rate of 60 mph.
1977 (summer)	Tuckerton	A mysterious creature makes eerie chopping noises, dents the side of a trailer, and leaves footprints at a campground here.
1978 (January)	Chatsworth	Several teenagers see the Jersey Devil. They say it has a bad odor and two large red eyes.
1978 (June)	Atsion	Two campers complain to rangers that the screaming of the Jersey Devil kept them awake all night.
1978 (summer)	Pine Barrens	Widespread areas of the Pine Barrens are swept by fires that last for many days. Some people say they were caused by the Jersey Devil.
1978 (fall)	Smithville Chestnut Neck	The Jersey Devil is heard howling at night.
1979 (May)	Tabernacle Township	A husband and wife report that the Jersey Devil is making horrible cries in the Pines.
1979 (summer)	Berkeley Township	A cat-like creature, called by some "The Jersey Devil," appears in the vicinity of the Robert Miller Air Park.
1979 (August)	Sussex County, DE	Footprints are seen in a number of locations, and one witness observes a kangaroo-like beast.
1979 (fall)	Pomona	Stockton State College students track the Jersey Devil after supposed sightings.
1980	New Egypt	The Jersey Devil is seen running across the road.
1980–81 (winter)	Waretown	The Jersey Devil bangs on sheds by houses along Barnegat Bay, frightening man and beast.
1981 (March)	Bass River Township	Citizens demand mayor's resignation after a Canadian newspaper claims the official said that local women were breeding with the Jersey Devil.
1981 (June)	Mullica River	A mysterious creature moves through the underbrush, following a group of canoers.

1981 (July)	Waretown	A group of young campers hears weird noises and sees the red eyes of the Jersey Devil peering through the darkness of the Pines.
1983 (fall)	Paisley	A couple hears terrible screams in the woods and describes them as sounding like a woman screaming.
1984 (fall)	Chatsworth	Screams are louder than chain saws and force woodcutters to leave a job.
1980s (late)	Vineland Area	Police, animal trappers, and others search the area after numerous incidents of howling and growling. In 1987, the remains of a badly mauled dog are found, surrounded by mysterious footprints. Many people attribute all of this to the work of the Jersey Devil.
1993 (fall)	Winslow Township	For a number of years up to 1993, a woman says, she heard and saw the Jersey Devil on her property. He usually arrived in the fall.
1995	Pompton Lakes	A strange creature is seen along Route 287. It has an armadillo-like face and is hopping in a manner similar to a kangaroo.
1995	New Gretna	A number of moving lights are seen just above the tops of pine trees.
1996 (October)	Sayreville	A motorist claims he saw the Jersey Devil flying over his car at night.

ACKNOWLEDGMENTS

The authors are greatly indebted to the many fine people who shared their experiences, tales, stories, and adventures with us. Below is a list of many of these contributors; any omissions on our part are accidental. Informants are usually listed by occupation or avocation, and the place cited is either of residence or employment at the time of contact. We take this opportunity to thank them all, from suppliers of brief but invaluable tidbits of information to those who willingly devoted hours of their valuable time. Needless to say, a book of this nature would be terribly hampered without such widespread and considerate assistance.

Elaine Abrahamson
Galloway Township
author

Gus Acevedo
Toms River

Luetta Leeds Adams
Somers Point

Jim Albertson
Mauricetown
folklorist, entertainer

Kathleen Anderson
Hammonton
Hammonton Public
Library

Richard Andwake
Blackwood
tattoo artist

Steve Badanis
Stockton
architect

Peggy Benham
balloonist

Clyde Birdsall
Sweetwater
retired forest ranger

Robert Blackwell
Newark
Newark Public Library

Jack E. Boucher
Linwood
photographer, historian

Andrew Broom
Barnegat
salt hay salesman

Ed Brown
Medford
journalist

Tom Brown, Jr.
Asbury
outdoorsman, author

Belva Browne
Barnegat
retired buyer

149

Watson Buck
Rancocas
antiquarian

David Burroughs
Medford Lakes
singer, the Jersey Devil
Barbershop Quartet

Rita Cassidy
Tuckerton
teacher, folklorist

Barry Cavileer
Lower Bank
volunteer fireman

Fred Cicetti
Leonia
journalist

Nels Clemenson
Estelle Manor City
campground owner,
former mayor

Mickey Coen
Forked River
naturalist

Rebecca B. Colesar
Trenton
New Jersey State Archives

Edward G. Cornman
Ocean City
bait and tackle shop
owner

Earl Danley
Burlington
forest ranger

Elizabeth Dannenhower
Haddonfield

Fritz Davis
Lambertville
editor, *The Jersey Devil*

Melona Davis
Cape May Court House
Cape May County Library

Walt Deetz
Barnegat
manager, the Jersey Devil
Women's Mud Wrestling
Team

John DeFeo
Malaga
New Jersey State Police

Lt. Michael E. Deibert
Atlantic City
New Jersey Air National
Guard

Anthony DeMarco
Hammonton
blueberry grower

Effie DeTroia
Brant Beach
realtor

Michael Dorofee
Tuckerton
glassblower

Peggy Dorsey
Ocean City
retail clerk

Tom Driscoll
Tuckerton

Billy Dunnkosky
Howell Township
musician

Sue Dupre
Princeton
health physicist

Edward Early
Plumstead Township
retired police chief

J.A. Edwards
Riverside
retired

Helen Fountaine
Whiting
poet

Louise Flink
Mays Landing
teacher

Mr. and Mrs. Philip Ford
Fort Pierce, FL

Robert Gaskill
Atsion
forest ranger

R.R. Geary
New York, NY
U.S. Coast Guard

Judith Gessel
Newton
Sussex County Library

Gary Giberson
Port Republic
wood carver

Angus Gillespie
New Brunswick
American Studies
Department,
Douglass College

Thomas Glenn, Jr.
Northfield
insurance agent

James J. Griffo
Madison
Provost, Fairleigh
Dickinson University,
Florham-Madison
Campus

J. Owen Grundy
Jersey City
Jersey City Public Library

Charles Haaf
Woodstown

Thomas Haaf
Woodstown
appliance store owner

Alice Haley
Monmouth Beach

Elizabeth C. Harrison
Collingswood

P.E. Hastings
Asbury Park
Asbury Park Press Library

Ken Hayek
Tuckerton
teacher

Scott Hazard
Tuckerton
campground owner

Edward O. Herbert, Jr.
Beachwood
Ocean County Sheriff's
Office

Mandy Herbert
Green Bank
retail clerk

David Higbee
Haddonfield
retired ship captain

Randy and Barbara
Higgenbottom
Paisley

Edith Hoelle
Woodbury
Gloucester County
Historical Society Library

Cornelius Hogenbirk
Waretown
photographer, writer

William Holton
Batsto
forest ranger

Larona Homer
Vincentown
author, retired teacher

Hugh Howard
Lakewood
Lakewood Public Library

Mr. and Mrs. Arba
  Hudson
Northfield

William W. Humbach
New York, NY
New York Times

Harry Hunt
Florence
circus owner

Ruth Hyde
Pleasant Mills

Mary Hysler
Leeds Point

Barbara S. Irwin
Newark
New Jersey Historical
Society Library

Ed Johnson
Millville
Holly City Bottle
Company

Shirley Johnson
Medford Lakes
costume shop owner

Robert E. Jones
Stanhope
Vestigia

Robert R. Jones
Pennsville
retired

Andy Kaff
Flushing, NY
collector

Mary Catherine Kennedy
Barnegat

C.F. Kier, Jr.
Oak Towne
Batsto Citizens Committee

Bill Kronmaier
Sweetwater
retired restaurant owner

William Kunze
Ship Bottom
contractor, fisherman,
journalist

Robert Kuppell
Leeds Point
retired restaurant owner

Elizabeth Lang
Moorestown

Herb Leeds
Leeds Point
wood carver

Wilmer Leeds
Oceanville

Michael Levitt
Philadelphia, PA
developer, fisherman

Andrea Lippi
Goshen
psychologist, folklorist

Lilli Lopez
Waretown
poet

Bessie LoSasso
Nesco

Jean LoSasso
Nesco
production worker

Mike Mangum
Toms River
naturalist

Dave Martino
Mount Holly
forest ranger

Daniel Leeds Mathews
Vincentown
retired businessman

Herb Mathis
New Gretna

William McMahon
Atlantic City
journalist, author

Mrlie Miss Kelly
Batsto
weaver

Bob Mitchell
Tuckerton

Florence Moore
Vincentown
clerk

Howard Mosley
Whiting
public utility worker

Robert Nisky
Manahawkin

Rose Norris
Nesco

Mr. and Mrs. George
 Norton
La Honda, CA

Cliff Oakley
Manahawkin
Wells Mills County Park

Pat Oleszko
New York, NY
costume designer

Sean O'Rourke
Toms River
naturalist

David G. Parris
Trenton
Natural Science,
New Jersey State Museum

Rosemary Philips
West Chester, PA
Chester County Historical
Society Library

Gary Piper
Tuckerton

Ann Plant
Madison
University Relations,
Fairleigh Dickinson
University,
Florham-Madison Campus

Mary Lou Ponsell
New Castle, DE
Wilmington College
Library

Louis Pozielli
Gibbstown
retired police chief

Bosh Pritchard
Vorhees Township
former Philadelphia Eagle,
publicist

Marion Puff
Sweetwater
bookstore clerk

Vic Raczka
New Gretna
restaurant owner

Linda Reddington
Manahawkin
writer, artist

Bill Reed
Trenton
producer and director,
New Jersey Educational
Television

Martha Mitchell Reider
Waretown
antique shop owner

Daniel Rich
New York, NY
bookstore owner

Arlene Ridgeway
Waretown
musician, author

Ron Rinaldi
Washington, D.C.
college student

Louis Rodia
Cape May Court House
publicist, writer

Charles Romano
Bellmawr

Walter Schumann
Camden Courier-Post
Sports Department

Christina M. Senezak
Newark
Newark Public Library

Ed Sheetz
Mays Landing
collector

Len Sheinkin
Atlantic City
publicist

Mildred Shubert
Wilmington, DE

Frances Shute
Oaklyn
Gloucester County
Historical Society

Edward Skipworth
New Brunswick
Rutgers University Library

Ray Smallwood
Newark, DE

Sara Smith
Wilmington, DE
social worker

Jack Stackhouse
Pitman

Ron F. Stephensen
Forked River
restaurant owner

Grace Stirnman
Bridgeton
Bridgeton Free Library

Pat Straub
Camden Courier-Post
Sports Department

Jeremiah J. Sullivan
Seattle, WA
University of Washington

Louis Sylvestro
Gibbstown
retired police chief

Lisa Thibault
Pemberton
Pinelands Preservation
Alliance

Bill Thompson
Narberth, PA

Mary Ann Thompson
Vincentown
cranberry grower

Thomas F. Tiernan
Metuchen
restaurant manager

Linda Tyrell
Haddonfield
store owner

Susan Vance
Atlantic County Library

Ann Waters
Swedesboro
newspaper publisher

Winslow Waters
Swedesboro
businessman

Charles Wells
Sicklerville

Debbie Will
Hammonton

Gladys Wilson
New Gretna
campground owner

Jack Wiseman
New Gretna
retired Mosquito Control
Commissioner

Renard Wiseman
New Gretna
volunteer fireman

Geraldine Witt
Penns Grove

BIBLIOGRAPHY

Books

Beck, Henry Charlton. *Jersey Genesis.* New Brunswick, NJ: Rutgers University Press, 1963.

Boucher, Jack E. *Absegami Yesteryear.* Somers Point, NJ: Atlantic County Historical Society, 1963.

Brown, Tom, Jr., and William Jon Watkins. *The Tracker.* Englewood Cliffs, NJ: Prentice-Hall, 1978.

Federal Writers' Project. *New Jersey: A Guide to its Past and Present.* New York: Viking, 1939.

Heston, Alfred. *Jersey Waggon Jaunts.* Atlantic County, NJ: Atlantic County Historical Society, 1926.

Hodge, F.W., ed. *Indian Notes and Monographs: Religion and Ceremony of the Lenape.* New York: M.R. Harrington, 1921.

Homer, Larona. *Blackbeard the Pirate and Other Stories of the Pine Barrens.* Wallingford, PA: Middle Atlantic Press, 1979.

Jagendorf, M.J. *Upstate, Downstate.* New York: Vanguard, 1949.

Kunze, William. *Shoreline Guide 1980.* Ship Bottom, NJ: William Kunze, 1980.

MacDougall, Curtis. *Hoaxes.* New York: Macmillan, 1940.

McCloy, James F., and Ray Miller, Jr. *The Jersey Devil.* Wallingford, PA: Middle Atlantic Press, 1976.

McMahon, William. *Historic Towne of Smithville.* Smithville, NJ: Historic Smithville Inn, 1967.

———. *South Jersey Towns.* New Brunswick, NJ: Rutgers University Press, 1973.

———. *Pine Barrens Legends, Lore and Lies.* Wallingford, PA: Middle Atlantic Press, 1980.

Mickle, Isaac. *Reminiscences of Old Gloucester Or Incidents in the History of the Counties of Gloucester, Atlantic and Camden, New Jersey.* 1845. Reprint, Woodbury, NJ: Gloucester County Historical Society, 1968.

Skinner, Charles. *American Myths and Legends.* Philadelphia: J.E. Lippincott, 1903.

Stillwell, John E. *Historical and Genealogical Miscellany: Early Settlers of New Jersey and their Descendants.* Vol. 3. Baltimore: Genealogical Publishing Company, 1970.

Young, Eugene L., and Elaine Conover Abrahamson. *The Story of Galloway Township 1774-1976.* Galloway Township: Galloway Township Bicentennial Committee, 1976.

Articles and Other Sources

Bontempo, Pat. "The Visits of the Hoodle-Doodle Bird: Re-Examining the 1909 Jersey Devil Sightings." *New Jersey Folklore*, vol. 2, no. 3 (spring 1981): 2-6.

Engle, Asa. Diary, 1/1/1857–8/31/1901. Photocopy. Gloucester County Historical Society.

Gillespie, Angus. "The Jersey Devil." *New Jersey Folklore*, vol. 1, no. 2 (spring 1977): 24-29.

———. "The Jersey Devil is in the Details." *New Jersey Outdoors* (fall 1993).

Guttman, Howard M. "The Legend of the Jersey Devil." *The Crossroads*, vol. 10, no. 4 (1973).

Halpert, Herbert. "Folktales and Legends from the New Jersey Pines: A Collection and a Study." Ph.D. dissertation, Indiana University, 1948.

Larner, Vance. Diary.

Leitch, Jackie, et al. "The Jersey Devil." *The Cockpit* (February–May 1967): 4-6.

Mayer, W.F. "In the Pines." *Atlantic Monthly* (May 1859).

McCloy, James, and Ray Miller, Jr. "The Jersey Devil." *New Jersey Folklore,* vol. 2, no. 2 (spring 1980): 11-12.

Moran, Peggy. "The Devil Made Me Do It." *Philadelphia Magazine* (December 1975).

Reed, Bill, producer. *Mother Leeds' Thirteenth Child.* New Jersey Public Broadcasting. Film.

Strasenburgh, Gordon R., Jr. "Perceptions and Images of the Wild Man." *Northwest Anthropological Research Notes*, vol. 9, no. 2 (1975): 281-298.

Sullivan, Jeremiah J., and James F. McCloy. "The Jersey Devil's Finest Hour." *New York Folklore Quarterly,* vol. 30 (September 1974): 231-238.

Tiede, Tom. "The Jersey Devil Is Back to Haunt Us." NEA Wire Service, October 1980.

Newspapers

American-Statesman (Houston, TX)
Asbury Park Press
Atlantic City Press
Burlington County Herald
Camden Courier-Post
Camden Post-Telegram
The Central Record (Medford, NJ)
Chester Times (Chester, PA)
The Coatesville Record (Coatesville, PA)
Daily Local News (West Chester, PA)
Daily Republican (Doylestown, PA)
Evening Bulletin (Philadelphia, PA)
Every Evening (Wilmington, DE)
Gloucester County Democrat
Light (San Antonio, TX)
London Times
The Morning News (Wilmington, DE)
National Examiner (Toronto, Canada)
New York Times
Newark News
Newark Star-Ledger
Newark Sun
Newark Sunday Call

News—San Antonio
North American (Philadelphia, PA)
Philadelphia Inquirer
Philadelphia Press
Philadelphia Public-Ledger
The Record (Paulsboro, NJ)
Rockland Independent (Nanuet, NY)
Salem Standard and Jerseyman
Salem Sunbeam
South Jersey Republican (Hammonton, NJ)
The Swedesboro News
Trenton Times
Trenton True American
Trentonian
Wall Street Journal
Woodbury Daily Times

Libraries

Atlantic County Library
Bridgeton Free Public Library
Bucks County Historical Society
Camden County Historical Society
Cape May County Library
Chester County Historical Society
Douglass College American Studies Department Folklore Collections
Free Library of Philadelphia
Gloucester County Historical Society
Hammonton Public Library
Lakewood Public Library
Millville Public Library
Monmouth County Historical Association
New Jersey Historical Society
New Jersey State Library
Newark Public Library
Ocean City Free Public Library
Rutgers University Library
Sussex County Library
Wilmington College Library

INDEX